decorative embellishments for
scrapbooks

32 Recipes for Enhancing Your Pages with New Techniques

QUARRY BOOKS

Trice Boerens

First published in the United States of America by
Quarry Books, an imprint of
Rockport Publishers, Inc.
33 Commercial Street
Gloucester, Massachusetts 01930-5089
Telephone: (978) 282-9590
Facsimile: (978) 283-2742
www.rockpub.com

Library of Congress Cataloging-in-Publication Data
Boerens, Trice.
    Decorative embellishments for scrapbooks : 32 recipes for enhancing your pages with
  new techniques / Trice Boerens.
        p.   cm.
    ISBN 1-59253-025-7 (pbk.)
    1. Photograph albums. 2. Photographs—Conservation and restoration. 3. Scrapbooks.
  4. Decoration and ornament. I. Title.
  TR465.B65 2004
    745.593—dc22   2003019746
                                                               CIP

ISBN 1-59253-025-7

10 9 8 7 6 5 4 3 2 1

Design: Yee Design
Project Manager: Karen Levy
Proofreader: Stacey Ann Follin
Photography: Brian Piper Photography

Printed in Singapore

contents

introduction

Do you want to make scrapbooking more interesting and also make your finished pages more attractive? Try combining familiar tools with uncommon materials when preserving the memories of special occasions and everyday events. *Decorative Embellishments for Scrapbooks* presents new scrapbooking techniques and introduces skills and materials used by fine artists, craft enthusiasts, and seamstresses. New scrapbooking techniques include shaping wire and quilling. Printing, gold leafing, and stenciling are new scrapbooking techniques borrowed from fine artists, and quilting and stitching use a needle and thread to add excitement to your pages.

This book includes 32 unique recipes. Each recipe is featured on two finished 12" x 12" (30.5 cm x 30.5 cm) pages, along with variations that can serve as springboards for your own creative interpretations.

These treatments are adapted for paper backdrops and can be executed in a few easy steps with easy-to-follow directions and informative photographs. The decorative elements are secondary, because these accents are designed to enhance your favorite photos rather than overpower them. Each completed page will become a pleasing composition that can be displayed in a frame or inserted into a cherished album. *Decorative Embellishments for Scrapbooks* will inspire the curious to begin creating scrapbooks and enable devoted scrappers to take their craft to the next level.

General Instructions

Many adhesives are available to use with this craft, and it is important to use glues that will not discolor the paper or cause it to disintegrate over time. Look for products that are archival quality to prevent future damage to the paper or the photos. Archival-quality adhesive spray is used with most of these recipes because it is convenient and can be applied evenly over most surfaces. Double-sided adhesive sheets are also used because they grip tightly and can be cut into any shape or configuration. Use nonstick scissors when working with this adhesive.

Take care to change the blades in your craft knife regularly. Trimming paper quickly dulls the metal blades, and dull blades will give your paper a ragged edge.

Because complete project instructions are provided for each recipe, specific photo sizes are listed. Of course, your featured photos may not be the same size or dimension, so you will need to make adjustments.

In each set of instructions, the smallest required size of colored paper listed is an 8^1/$_2$" x 11" (21.5 cm x 28 cm) sheet. Sort through your paper scraps, and if the scrap sizes correspond to the template sizes, feel free to use them.

All measurements in the instructions are listed as width x length.

Folded Borders

Paper is everywhere in our lives and has become so commonplace that its beauty and versatility are sometimes unappreciated. Scrapbook enthusiasts, however, regard paper as a treasure and delight in transforming it into art. Use folding to make paper borders that virtually jump off the page. These folded-paper flowers add dimension without adding bulk. A few well-placed folds and a little sleight of hand can turn a paper square into a beautiful blossom. In fact, two of these flower variations begins with a simple square.

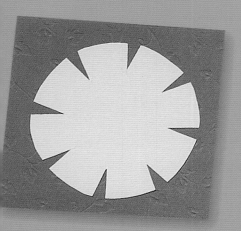

Sample 1: To make a folded flower, cut out the center flower shape.

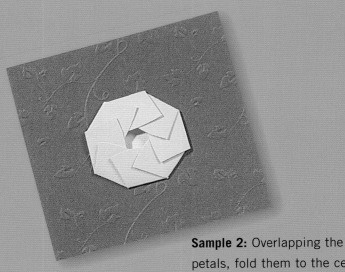

Sample 2: Overlapping the petals, fold them to the center of the flower.

Sample 3: Layer the flat and folded shapes, then attach them to the page.

Sorority Sisters

Throw open the windows and let the outside in with this happy border of morning glories.

Materials

- photos
- one 12" x 12" (30.5 cm x 30.5 cm) sheet purple paper
- one 12" x 12" (30.5 cm x 30.5 cm) sheet cream paper
- one 8 1/2" x 11" (21.5 cm x 28 cm) sheet blue patterned paper with white reverse side
- one 8 1/2" x 11" (21.5 cm x 28 cm) sheet green patterned paper
- one 8 1/2" x 11" (21.5 cm x 28 cm) sheet yellow paper
- white quilling paper
- turquoise micro beads
- archival-quality adhesive spray
- double-sided adhesive sheet, such as Peel-N-Stick

Tools

- metal-edged ruler
- craft knife
- scissors
- pencil
- tracing paper
- kneaded rubber eraser
- black fine-tip marker

Instructions

1. With the ruler and knife, trim the cream paper to 9 1/2" x 12" (24 cm x 30.5 cm). Tear the right edge of the rectangle. Place the cream paper 2 3/8" (6 cm) from the left edge of the purple paper. Using a pencil, lightly mark the purple paper at the left edge of the cream paper for placement. Following the manufacturer's directions for the adhesive spray, coat the back of the cream paper. Press in place.

2. Using the scissors, trim the photos to the following sizes, clockwise from left: 2 1/2" x 4 1/4" (6.5 cm x 11 cm), 5 1/8" x 2 3/4" (13 cm x 7 cm), and 4" x 6" (10 cm x 15 cm). Place the small photo 2" (5 cm) from the left edge and 3 1/2" (9 cm) from the bottom edge of the purple paper. Place the top photo 2 3/4" (7 cm) from the right edge of the purple paper and 5/8" (1.5 cm) from the top edge of the cream paper. Place the bottom photo 3" (7.5 cm) from the right edge of the purple paper and 3/4" (2 cm) from the bottom edge of the cream paper. Mark the cream paper at the corners of the photos for placement. Coat the backs of the photos with adhesive spray. Press in place.

3. From the yellow paper, cut one 1/4" x 11" (0.6 cm x 28 cm) strip. Loosely wrap one or two lengths of quilling paper around the yellow strip. Press the quilling paper flat. From the double-sided adhesive sheet, cut one 1/8" x 9" (0.3 cm x 23 cm) strip. Peel off the protective paper, and attach the adhesive sheet to the back of the yellow strip. Mark a vertical line on the cream paper 1 1/8" (3 cm) from the right edge of the purple paper. From the quilling paper, cut six 2" (5 cm) lengths. Place them at various angles on the marked line. Remove the remaining protective paper from the adhesive sheet, and press the wrapped strip in place on the marked line.

4. Using the tracing paper, make the template for the leaf shape. From the green patterned paper, cut five leaf shapes. From the double-sided adhesive sheet, cut five 1/2" (1 cm) squares. Peel off the protective paper, and attach the squares to the backs of the leaf shapes. Remove the remaining protective paper. Referring to the photo for placement, press the leaf shapes in place. From the blue-and-white patterned paper, cut one 1 3/4" (4.5 cm) square. Referring to Diagram A, fold the corners of the square into the center. Trim the center corners to

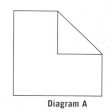

Leaf Template (Photocopy at 100%)

Diagram A

make a small window. Trim the folded corners. Cut a small rectangle from the double-sided adhesive sheet. Peel off the protective paper, and attach the adhesive sheet to the center of the flower. Remove the remaining protective paper from the adhesive sheet. Sprinkle the exposed adhesive sheet with the micro beads, removing any excess beads. Repeat to make four more flowers. From the double-sided adhesive sheet, cut five 1/2" (1 cm) squares. Peel off the protective paper, and attach the adhesive sheet to the backs of the flowers. Remove the remaining protective paper. Referring to the photo for placement, press the flowers on the leaf shapes. Trim the ends of the quilling paper, if necessary.

5. Using the marker, write the title. Using the kneaded rubber eraser, remove all pencil marks.

Paris in Springtime

The climbing paper vines lead the eye up, as does the spire in the photo.

Paris in the Springtime, 2003

Materials

- photo
- one 12" x 12" (30.5 cm x 30.5 cm) sheet blue paper
- one 8 1/2" x 11" (21.5 cm x 28 cm) sheet green paper with white reverse side
- one 8 1/2" x 11" (21.5 cm x 28 cm) sheet pink paper
- one 8 1/2" x 11" (21.5 cm x 28 cm) white paper
- one 8 1/2" x 11" (21.5 cm x 28 cm) sheet yellow patterned paper
- white quilling paper
- archival-quality adhesive spray
- double-sided adhesive sheet, such as Peel-N-Stick
- red pencil
- pink pencil

Tools

- metal-edged ruler
- craft knife
- scissors
- pencil
- tracing paper
- kneaded rubber eraser
- black fine-tip marker (optional)

Instructions

1. Using the ruler and knife, trim the photo to 7 3/8" x 9 1/4" (18.5 cm x 23.5 cm). Place the photo 1 1/4" (3 cm) from the left edge and 5/8" (1.5 cm) from the top edge of the blue paper. With the pencil, lightly mark the blue paper at the corners of the photo for placement. Following the manufacturer's directions, coat the back of the photo with adhesive spray. Press in place.

2. From the yellow patterned paper, cut one 1/4" x 11" (0.6 cm x 28 cm) strip. Loosely wrap one or two lengths of quilling paper around the yellow strip. Press the quilling paper flat. From the double-sided adhesive sheet, cut one 1/8" x 9" (0.3 cm x 23 cm) strip. Peel off the protective paper, and attach the adhesive sheet to the back of the yellow strip. Mark a vertical line 1 1/4" (3 cm) from the right edge of the blue paper. Remove the remaining protective paper from the adhesive sheet, and press the wrapped strip in place on the marked line.

3. From the pink paper, cut one 1 3/4" (4.5 cm) square. Draw a diagonal line on the square from the bottom-left corner to the top-right corner. Referring to Diagram A, fold the bottom right corner of the square into the center to meet the marked line. Fold the top left corner of the square into the center at the marked line. Referring to Diagram B, fold the top-right corner in 1/4" (0.6 cm). Use the kneaded rubber eraser to erase the line. Use the scissors to trim the bottom-left corner. Using the red pencil, draw one or two small circles beneath the folded corner. Repeat to make two more pink flowers. From the green-and-white paper, cut one 3/8" x 3 1/2" (1 cm x 9 cm) strip. With the white side facing up, wrap the strip around the bottom of one flower, and angle the ends up behind the flower. Trim the ends of the strip, if necessary. Repeat with the remaining two flowers. From the double-sided adhesive sheet, cut three 1/2" (1 cm) squares. Peel off the protective paper, and attach the squares to the backs of the flowers and the leaves. Remove the remaining protective paper. Referring to the photo for placement, press the flowers in place.

4. From the white paper, cut one 1 1/2" (4 cm) square. Fold the corners of the square into the center. Trim the center corners to make a small window. Unfold the white square. From the green-and-white paper, cut one 1/2" (1 cm) square. From the double-sided adhesive sheet, cut one

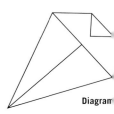

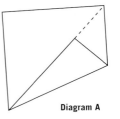

Diagram A

Diagram

1/4" (0.6 cm) square. Peel off the protective paper, and attach the square to the back of the green square. Remove the remaining protective paper from the adhesive sheet, and press the square in place in the center of the white square. Refold the paper, and fold the corners in 1/4" (0.6 cm). Repeat to make three more white flowers. From the double-sided adhesive sheet, cut four 1/2" (1 cm) squares. Peel off the protective paper, and attach the squares to the backs of the white flowers. Remove the remaining protective paper. Referring to the photo for placement, press the flowers in place.

5. On the white paper, print the title using the black marker (or do this on a computer). Trim the title box to 7" x 3/4" (18 cm x 2 cm). Coat the back of the title box with adhesive spray. Referring to the photo for placement, press the title box in place.

6. Use the kneaded rubber eraser to remove all pencil marks.

Paper Clay

Lightweight, air-hardening modeling clays are widely available and are perfect for enhancing scrapbooks with simple sculptural shapes. The material can be molded and shaped while it's still moist, and it air-dries naturally without needing to be baked or fired in a kiln. Once the clay is dry, it can be painted with tempera, watercolor, or acrylic paint. These nontoxic clays contain all-natural ingredients and can be used by people of any skill level. They are available in a wide range of blendable colors, from natural stone and marble tints to brights, pearlescents, and metallics. The samples here show some of the many techniques that can be applied to air-hardening clay.

Sample 1: Trace and cut out a simple leaf shape from rolled-out clay. Embed a piece of plastic-coated wire as the stem, and let dry.

Sample 2: Use pinking shears or other decorative scissors to cut a simple square from rolled-out clay. Embed coins or other found objects, and let dry.

Sample 3: Use decorative scissors to cut a border from rolled-out clay. Press in buttons. Use a pencil tip to imprint the background with dots. Let dry.

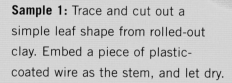

Little Cowboys

In this page design, the acorn clay tiles illustrate the quote, adding a horizontal design element that nicely balances the vertical silhouette of the tree.

Materials

- photo
- one 12" x 12" (30.5 cm x 30.5 cm) sheet mustard paper
- one 12" x 12" (30.5 cm x 30.5 cm) sheet cream paper
- one 9" x 12" (23 cm x 30.5 cm) sheet black textured paper
- one die-cut tree shape or one 12" x 12" (30.5 cm x 30.5 cm) sheet light brown paper
- air-hardening modeling clay, such as PaperClay
- acorn rubber stamp with $1^{3}/_{8}$" x $1^{3}/_{8}$" (3.5 cm x 3.5 cm) image size
- tan acrylic craft paint
- double-sided adhesive sheet, such as Peel-N-Stick
- four self-adhesive foam spacers
- brown chisel-point marker
- archival-quality adhesive spray

Tools

- waxed paper
- rolling pin
- craft knife
- metal-edged ruler
- pencil
- kneaded rubber eraser
- fine-grain sandpaper
- tan acrylic craft paint
- white craft glue
- paintbrush
- paper towel
- tracing paper (optional)

Instructions

1. Using the rolling pin, roll the clay on the waxed paper to approximately $^{1}/_{8}$" (0.3 cm) thick. (Trimmed clay tiles are $1^{7}/_{8}$" (5 cm) square, so create enough surface area for three tiles.) Press the stamp in the clay three times, allowing $^{1}/_{2}$" (1 cm) around each image. Let dry.

2. Center the images, and using the ruler and knife, cut out three $1^{7}/_{8}$" (5 cm) square tiles. Dried clay is dense and requires several passes with the knife. Use the sandpaper to slightly sand the edges.

3. Dilute the acrylic craft paint to approximately three parts water to one part paint. Paint the tiles. Blot the tiles with the paper towel, if necessary. Let dry. Apply one light coat of craft glue to the backs of the tiles to seal. Let dry.

4. Place the die-cut tree shape on the center-left of the mustard paper. Or, using the tracing paper, make the template for the tree shape. (See Tree template on page 102.) From the light brown paper, cut one tree shape. Use the pencil to mark lightly the mustard paper at chosen reference points on the tree for placement. Following the manufacturer's directions, coat the back of the tree with adhesive spray. Press in place.

5. Using the ruler and knife, cut one 12" x $1^{3}/_{4}$" (30.5 cm x 4.5 cm) strip from the cream paper. Place the strip $1^{1}/_{4}$" (3.5 cm) from the bottom edge of the mustard paper. Mark the mustard paper at the top edge of the strip for placement. Coat the back of the strip with adhesive spray. Press in place.

6. From the double-sided adhesive sheet, cut three $1^{1}/_{2}$" (4 cm) squares. Peel off the protective paper, and attach the squares to the backs of the clay tiles. Remove the remaining protective paper from the adhesive sheet. Center one tile on the cream strip, and press in place. Attach the remaining tiles, allowing $1^{3}/_{4}$" (4.5 cm) between each.

7. Using the ruler and knife, trim the photo to $3^{1}/_{2}$" x $5^{5}/_{8}$" (9 cm x 14 cm). Coat the back of the photo with the adhesive spray. Place the photo on the black paper, and press to adhere. Centering the photo, trim the black paper to 4" x $6^{1}/_{8}$" (10 cm x 15.5 cm). Place the mounted photo $2^{1}/_{4}$" (6 cm) from the left edge and $2^{1}/_{2}$" (6.5 cm) from the top edge of the mustard paper. Use the pencil to mark the mustard paper at the corners of the mounted photo for placement. Attach the foam spacers to the back of the black paper at the corners. Peel the protective paper from the foam spacers, and press the photo in place.

8. Use the marker to write the quote, names, and date.

9. Use the kneaded rubber eraser to remove all pencil marks.

Western Vistas

The organic swirl shapes in the clay border echo the natural curves of the clouds and mountaintops in the photos. The white clay highlights the white, handwritten captions.

Materials

- photos
- one 12" x 12" (30.5 cm x 30.5 cm) sheet dark brown paper
- air-hardening modeling clay, such as PaperClay
- swirl stamp with $1\,^1/_2$" x $1\,^1/_2$" (4 cm x 4 cm) image size
- white pencil
- double-sided adhesive sheet, such as Peel-N-Stick
- archival-quality adhesive spray

Tools

- waxed paper
- rolling pin
- craft knife
- metal-edged ruler
- pencil
- kneaded rubber eraser
- white craft glue
- fine-grain sandpaper

Instructions

1. Using the rolling pin, roll the clay on the waxed paper to approximately $^1/_8$" (0.3 cm) thick. Press the stamp in the clay in a random pattern within a 2" x 12" (5 cm x 30.5 cm) surface area. Let dry.

2. Using the ruler and knife, trim one side of the clay to create a straight border. Dried clay is dense and requires several passes with the knife. Use the knife to trim carefully around the swirls on the opposite side of the border. Use the sandpaper to sand the edges of the trimmed border lightly. Apply one light coat of craft glue to the back of the clay border to seal. Let dry.

3. Using the ruler and knife, trim the photos to 7" x 3 $^3/_8$" (18 cm x 8.5 cm). Place the top photo 2 $^1/_8$" (5.5 cm) from the right edge, and $^5/_8$" (1.5 cm) from the top edge of the brown paper. Center the remaining photos under the top photo, allowing $^3/_8$" (1 cm) between each. Use the pencil to lightly mark the brown paper at the corners of the photos for placement. Following the manufacturer's directions, coat the backs of the photos with adhesive spray. Press in place.

4. Using the white pencil, write the captions.

5. From the double-sided adhesive sheet, cut one shape that matches the clay border. Peel off the protective paper, and attach the adhesive shape to the back of the clay border. Remove the remaining protective paper, and attach the clay border to the right edge of the brown paper.

6. Use the kneaded rubber eraser to remove all pencil marks.

recipe
3

Fusible Fabric Appliqué

For centuries, appliqué has been the favorite pastime of quilters. Combine the variety of available fabrics with the versatility of the technique, and the design possibilities are endless. However the traditional needle-turn method is time-consuming and requires many tiny hand stitches. With the introduction of fusible web, fast and easy iron-on appliqué is now possible. Fusible web is paper-backed adhesive that is activated by the heat from an iron. It is sold by the yard in craft and fabric stores. Patterns can be drawn on the smooth, paper side of the web. The rough side is coated with adhesive crystals that melt when heated by a hot iron. Fusible web enables scrapbook enthusiasts to make fabric appliqués by fusing fabric to paper and then attaching the paper-backed appliqués to the page. Designs can be ironed directly onto the page, but, unfortunately, the heat from the iron can warp the paper. Experiment with mixing patterns and textures of interesting fabrics to enhance your pages.

Sample 1. Use cheery pink fabric to line this puffy paper envelope.

Sample 2. Snip many tiny squares from fabric that has first been fused to paper. Then construct this patchwork quilt to enhance a photo of your favorite baby.

Sample 3. Make a statement. Cut letters or numbers from fused fabric and string them together for titles or captions.

Art Deco Flowers

Fabric absorbs more light and has a softer-appearing surface than paper. To stabilize the fabric and achieve a clean-cut edge, fused the paper to the wrong side of the fabric. After fusing, cut the fabric into curvy silhouette shapes, such as these Art Deco flowers.

Materials

- photo
- one 12" x 12" (30.5 cm x 30.5 cm) sheet wine paper
- one 8 1/2" x 11" (21.5 cm x 28 cm) sheet burgundy paper
- one 8 1/2" x 11" (21.5 cm x 28 cm) sheet gray vellum
- two sheets typing paper
- scrap burgundy print fabric
- scrap green print fabric
- 4 1/2" (11.5 cm) fusible web
- archival-quality adhesive spray
- double-sided adhesive sheet, such as Peel-N-Stick

Tools

- craft knife
- metal-edged ruler
- pencil
- iron
- scissors
- kneaded rubber eraser

Instructions

1. From the fusible web, cut one 4 1/2" x 7" (11.5 cm x 18 cm) rectangle. From the green fabric, cut one 5" x 7 1/2" (12.5 cm x 19 cm) rectangle. Following the manufacturer's directions, center and fuse the web to the wrong side of the green fabric. Let cool. On the typing paper, trace three stems 1/4" (0.6 cm) apart. (See Flower template on page 102.) Because the typing paper is on the back of the fabric appliqués, all templates are reversed. Peel the protective paper from the web. Place the fabric, adhesive side up, on the ironing surface. Center the stems on the fabric, and use an iron to fuse the typing paper to the fabric. Let cool. Cut out the stems.

2. From the fusible web, cut one 1 1/2" x 4" (4 cm x 25.5 cm) rectangle. From the burgundy fabric, cut one 2" x 4 1/2" (5 cm x 11.5 cm) rectangle. Center and fuse the web to the wrong side of the burgundy fabric. Let cool. Trace three flowers 1/4" (0.6 cm) apart on the typing paper. Peel

the protective paper from the web. Place the fabric, adhesive side up, on the ironing surface. Center the flowers and fuse the typing paper to the fabric. Let cool. Cut out the flower sections.

3. Place one stem 1 5/8" (4 cm) from the left edge and 3/4" (2 cm) from the bottom edge of the wine paper. Align them horizontally, and place the remaining two stems on the wine paper, allowing 1" (2.5 cm) between each stem. Use the pencil to mark lightly the wine paper at the top and the bottom of each stem for placement. Following the manufacturer's directions, coat the backs of the stems with the adhesive spray. Press in place. Coat the backs of the flower sections with the adhesive spray. Press in place.

4. Using the ruler and the knife, trim the photo to 4 1/2" x 6 3/4" (11.5 cm x 17 cm). Coat the back of the photo with the adhesive spray. Place the photo on the burgundy paper, and press. Centering the photo, trim the burgundy paper to 4 3/4" x

7" (12 cm x 18 cm). Place the mounted photo 1 1/4" (3 cm) from the right edge and 1 1/2" (4 cm) from the top edge of the wine paper. Use the pencil to mark the wine paper at the corners of the mounted photo for placement. Coat the back of the burgundy paper with the adhesive spray. Press in place.

5. Use the pencil to print a message on the gray vellum. Trim the gray vellum to 3 1/4" x 2" (8.5 cm x 5 cm). From the double-sided adhesive sheet, cut four small triangles. Peel off the protective paper, and attach the adhesive sheet to the corners of the message box. Remove the remaining protective paper from the adhesive sheet. Align the message box with the right side of the mounted photo, and press it in place below the photo.

6. Use the kneaded rubber eraser to remove all pencil marks.

Fused Frame

This combination of vintage fabrics creates a tactile, textured frame that enhances the antique quality of this family photo. The buttons echo the paper pattern and add a three-dimensional appeal to the presentation.

Materials

- photo
- one 12" x 12" (30.5 cm x 30.5 cm) sheet blue patterned paper
- one 8 1/2" x 11" (21.5 cm x 28 cm) sheet oatmeal paper
- one sheet typing paper
- 1/4 yard (23 cm) blue print fabric
- 1/4 yard (23 cm) blue velveteen fabric
- 1/4 yard (23 cm) fusible web
- double-sided adhesive sheet, such as Peel-N-Stick
- archival-quality tape
- three assorted buttons
- blue thread
- white milky pen

Tools

- craft knife
- metal-edged ruler
- pencil
- iron
- scissors
- needle
- kneaded rubber eraser

Instructions

1. From the fusible web, cut one 8" x 10" (20.5 cm x 25.5 cm) rectangle. From the blue print fabric, cut one 8 1/2" x 10 1/2" (21.5 cm x 26.5 cm) rectangle. Center the web, and, following the manufacturer's instructions, use the iron to fuse the web to the wrong side of the blue print fabric. Let cool. Referring to Diagram A, draw a frame on the typing paper. Peel the protective paper from the web. Place the fabric, adhesive side up, on the ironing surface. Center the frame on the fabric, and use the iron to fuse the typing paper to the fabric. Let cool. Cut out the frame.

2. Draw the scalloped border for the frame on the paper side of the fusible web. (See Scalloped Frame Border template on page 103.) Use the scissor to cut around the border, allowing 1/2" (1 cm) around the marked lines. Use the iron to fuse the border piece to the wrong side of the velveteen fabric. Let cool. Using the scissors, cut the scalloped border along the marked lines. Peel the protective paper from the fusible web. Place the blue print frame, right side up, on the ironing surface. Place the border, right side up, on the frame. Align the inside of the border with the inside of the frame, and use the iron to fuse the border to the frame. Let cool.

3. Place the fabric frame 1 1/2" (4 cm) from the right edge and 1" (2.5 cm) from the top edge of the blue paper. Use the pencil to mark lightly the blue paper at the corners of the frame for placement. Following the manufacturer's directions, coat the back of the frame with the adhesive spray. Press in place.

4. Using the ruler and the knife, trim the photo to 6 5/8" x 4 3/4" (17 cm x 12 cm). Coat the back of the photo with the adhesive spray. Center the photo in the frame, and press to adhere.

5. Using the needle and the thread, stitch one button to the top-left corner of the frame. From the oatmeal paper, cut two circles that are slightly larger in diameter than the remaining buttons. Referring to the photo for placement, stitch circles and buttons to the frame and the blue paper. With the tape, square the ends of thread to the back of the paper.

6. Use the pen to write the caption.

7. Use the kneaded rubber eraser to remove all pencil marks.

Diagram A

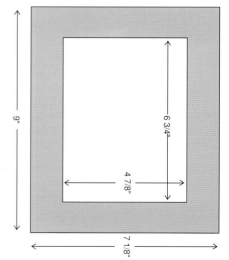

Silk Flower Appliqué

The ubiquitous silk flower can easily dress up any page. Take the flower apart, and attach the petals and leaves to the paper using fusible web or double-sided adhesive. Or stitch the flower parts to a scrap of fabric, and attach the fabric to the paper. Silk petals and leaves are more durable than paper, are articulated with fine detail, and are colored with lovely variegated shading.

Sample 1. Layer petals and leaves randomly on gauzy ribbon. Machine-stitch through all layers using contrasting thread.

Sample 3. Arrange petals and leaves to create an individual flower. Secure with a satin-stitched center.

Sample 2. Gather petals with a running stitch to make three-dimensional blossoms, and attach them to a satin ribbon.

Swing Time

The leaves and petals of silk flowers can be configured to create butterflies, hummingbirds, and even fairies.

Materials

- photo
- one 12" x 12" (30.5 cm x 30.5 cm) sheet yellow paper
- one 8 1/2" x 11" (21.5 cm x 28 cm) sheet gray paper
- one 8 1/2" x 11" (21.5 cm x 28 cm) sheet cream patterned paper
- one 2" x 4" (5 cm x 10 cm) scrap gold moiré fabric
- one 4" x 5" (10 cm x 12.5 cm) scrap light blue fabric
- one 3" x 3" (7.5 cm x 7.5 cm) scrap medium blue fabric
- gold felt
- one pair small silk leaves, approximately 1" (2.5 cm) from tip to tip—Note: All leaf pairs are connected in the center.
- two pair medium silk leaves, approximately 2 1/2" (6.5 cm) from tip to tip
- one pair large silk leaves, approximately 3" (7.5 cm) from tip to tip
- one yellow silk flower, 1" (2.5 cm) in diameter
- four blue silk flowers, 1" (2.5 cm) in diameter
- two pink silk flowers, 2" (5 cm) in diameter
- blue thread
- blue embroidery floss
- gray embroidery floss
- one tan 1/10" (0.3 cm) chenille stem
- archival-quality adhesive spray
- black fine-tip marker (optional)

Tools

- metal-edged ruler
- craft knife
- tracing paper
- needle
- scissors

Instructions

1. Using the ruler and knife, trim the photo to 6 3/4" x 7 3/4" (17 cm x 20 cm). Coat the back with adhesive spray. Place on the gray paper; press to adhere. Center the photo, and trim the gray paper to 7 1/4" x 8 1/4" (18.5 cm x 21 cm). Place the mounted photo 1/2" (1 cm) from the right edge and 3/8" (1 cm) from the top edge of the yellow paper. With a pencil mark the yellow paper at the corners for placement. Coat the back with adhesive spray. Press in place.

2. Use the marker or a computer to print the poem on the cream patterned paper. Center the poem, and trim the paper to 6 7/8" x 2 3/8" (17.5 cm x 6 cm). Trim a separate strip of paper and print the author's name on it. Place the poem 7/8" (2 cm) from the left edge and 7/8" (2 cm) from the bottom edge of the yellow paper. Mark the yellow paper at the corners for placement. Coat the back with adhesive spray. Press in place. Coat the back of the author's name; press in place.

3. From the gold moiré fabric, cut one 1 3/4" x 3 1/2" (4.5 cm x 9 cm) rectangle. Referring to the photo for placement, layer one pair

Dress Template

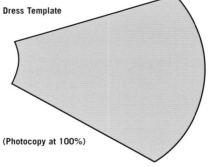

(Photocopy at 100%)

of 2 1/2" (6.5 cm) leaves and two blue flowers on the rectangle. With blue thread, stitch through the flower centers to secure. Repeat for the second flower. Place the fabric 1 3/4" (4.5 cm) from the right edge and 3/4" (2 cm) from the top edge of the yellow paper. Mark the yellow paper at the corners for placement. Coat the back with adhesive spray. Press in place.

4. From the light blue fabric, cut one 3 1/2" x 4 3/4" (9 cm x 12 cm) rectangle. Use the tracing paper to make the dress template. From the medium blue fabric, cut one dress shape. From the gold felt, cut one circle, 7/8" (2 cm) in diameter. Referring to Diagram A and the light blue rectangle,

layer the large leaves, stems, and dress. With blue thread, stitch around the outer edge of the dress to secure. Layer the small leaves, flower, and face. Stitch around the outer edge of the face to secure. Fold the top third of the pink flowers over to create a ruffled skirt. Place them side-by-side at the bottom of the dress; stitch through all layers to secure. Using two strands of gray embroidery floss, stitch the eyes, nose, and mouth. Using three strands of blue embroidery floss, stitch shoes. Place the fabric 1/4" (0.6 cm) from the right edge and 1/4" (6 cm) from the bottom edge of the yellow paper. Mark the yellow paper at the corners for placement. Coat the back with adhesive spray. Press in place. Use the eraser to remove pencil marks.

Diagram A

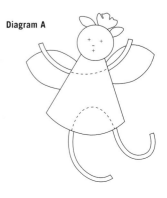

'50s Kids

The versatility of silk flowers is demonstrated on this page. The same blue petals and small leaves are used for both the framed vignette and the bookmark.

Materials

- photo
- one 12" x 12" (30.5 cm x 30.5 cm) sheet black embossed paper
- one 8 1/2" x 11" (21.5 cm x 28 cm) sheet handmade paper
- one 8 1/2" x 11" (21.5 cm x 28 cm) sheet silver paper
- one 8 1/2" x 11" (21.5 cm x 28 cm) sheet black paper
- two pair medium silk leaves, approximately 2 1/2"" (6.5 cm) from tip to tip
- one pair large silk leaves, approximately 3" (7.5 cm) from tip to tip
- one yellow silk flower, 1 1/2" (4 cm) in diameter
- seven blue silk flowers, 1" (2.5 cm) in diameter
- seven individual leaves, 1" (2.5 cm) in length
- 3/4" (2 cm)-wide green velvet ribbon, 6" (15 cm) long
- 1 1/2" (3.8 cm)-wide cream sheer ribbon, 6" (15 cm) long
- double-sided adhesive sheet, such as Peel-N-Stick
- archival-quality adhesive spray
- archival-quality tape
- green thread
- white pencil

Tools

- metal-edged ruler
- craft knife
- scissors
- white craft glue
- sewing machine

Instructions

1. Using the ruler and knife, trim the silver paper to 4 1/2" x 6" (11.5 cm x 15 cm). Center the rectangle, and use the knife to cut a 3 1/4" x 4 3/4" (8 cm x 12 cm) window to make a mat. Place the mat 3/4" (0.6 cm) from the right edge and 1/2" (1 cm) from the bottom edge of the black paper. Use the pencil to lightly mark the black paper at the corners of the mat for placement. Following the manufacturer's directions, coat the back of the mat with the adhesive spray. Press in place.

2. Using a silk leaf as a template, cut three leaves from the double-sided adhesive sheet. Peel off the protective paper, and attach the adhesive sheet to the backs of three silk leaves. Refer to the photo for placement of the leaves and the blossoms within the silver mat. Remove the remaining protective paper, and attach the leaves to the black paper. Repeat this process for the yellow flower and three blue flowers. From the silver paper, cut 1/8" (0.3 cm) strips. Trim the strips to make the stems.

Coat the backs of the stems with adhesive spray. Press in place. Trim small pieces from the strip to make the flower centers. Apply a small amount of white craft glue to the backs of the flower centers. Press them in place.

3. Trim the photo to 7 1/4" x 5 1/4" (18.5 cm x 13.5 cm). Trim the handmade paper to 7 3/4" x 5 3/4" (20 cm x 14.5 cm). Center and cut a 6 1/4" x 4 1/4" (16 cm x 11 cm) window to make a mat. Use the archival-quality tape to attach the photo to the back of the mat. Place the matted photo 1" (2.5 cm) from the left edge and 1/2" (1 cm) from the edge of the black paper. Use the pencil to mark the black paper at the corners of the matted photo for placement. Coat the back of the matted photo with the adhesive spray. Press in place.

4. Center and layer the ribbons, leaves, and flowers in the following order: sheer ribbon, leaves, velvet ribbon, and two layers of flowers. Pin in place. Machine-stitch through all layers down the center of the

layered ribbon. Referring to the photo, trim the top and bottom of the stitched ribbon. From the double-sided adhesive, cut one 1/2" x 3" (1 cm x 7.5 cm) strip. Peel off the protective paper, and attach the adhesive sheet to the back of the stitched ribbon. Remove the remaining protective paper, and attach the stitched ribbon to the black paper, along the right edge of the matted photo.

5. Using the white pencil, write the caption on the black paper. Center the caption box, and trim it to the desired size. Coat the back of the caption box with the adhesive spray, and press in place beneath the photo.

6. Use the kneaded rubber eraser to remove all pencil marks.

recipe #

5

Shaped Wire

Papercrafters have discovered that they can draw and write with malleable wire, almost as easily as they can with a pencil or pen. Become familiar with the tractability of wire, and let your imagination run wild. Drawing with wire is similar to drawing on an Etch-A-Sketch—the best designs consist of one continuous line. Wire messages or images add a particular attitude of whimsy to any scrapbook project. The downside to attaching shaped wire to paper is that the contact area is small and craft glues don't hold well. A better solution is to back the wire with thin strips of double-sided adhesive or to anchor the wire with strips of paper. Also, note that fragile papers or photos on a facing page may be scratched by the wire, so position your wire embellishments strategically.

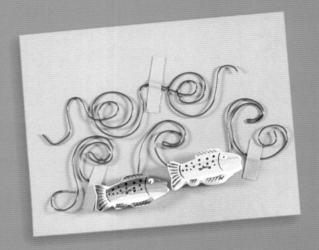

Sample 1. Thread wooden fish buttons onto 24-gauge green wire. Then use needle-nose pliers to shape the wire to simulate the movement of ocean waves.

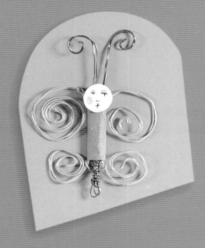

Sample 2. Bundle wire together to form a body. Then turn and twist yellow and purple 24-gauge wire to fashion this butterfly.

Sample 3. Shape a short holiday message from shiny 20-gauge copper wire. The wire is anchored with paper strips, which have been drawn through slits to the back of the page.

18 Decorative Embellishments for **Scrapbooks**

Cooking

These playful spoons feature centers that are coiled tightly. The more wire that is used in fashioning an object, the more solid that object will appear.

Materials

- photo
- one 12" x 12" (30.5 cm x 30.5 cm) sheet brown paper
- one 8¹⁄₂" x 11" (21.5 cm x 28 cm) sheet peach patterned paper
- one 8¹⁄₂" x 11" (21.5 cm x 28 cm) sheet gold patterned paper
- one 8¹⁄₂" x 11" (21.5 cm x 28 cm) sheet ivory paper
- archival-quality adhesive spray
- red 20-gauge coated wire
- blue 24-gauge coated wire
- black acrylic craft paint
- double-sided adhesive sheet, such as Peel-N-Stick

Tools

- craft knife
- metal-edged ruler
- pencil
- tracing paper
- fine paintbrush
- needle-nose pliers
- wire cutters
- scissors

Instructions

1. Using the ruler and knife, trim the large photo to 5¹⁄₂" x 4¹⁄₄" (14 cm x 11 cm). Following the manufacturer's directions, coat the back of the photo with the adhesive spray. Place the photo on the peach patterned paper, and press to adhere. Center the photo, and trim the peach paper to 6" x 4³⁄₄" (15 cm x 12 cm). Center and place the mounted photo at an angle on the brown paper, with the left corner 1³⁄₄" (4.5 cm) and the right corner 1¹⁄₄" (3.5 cm) from the top edge of the paper. Use the pencil to lightly mark the brown paper at the corners of the photo for placement. Coat the back of the mounted photo with adhesive spray. Press in place.

2. Use the tracing paper to make the hat template. From the ivory paper, cut the desired number of chef's hats. (See Hat template on page 102. Hat size may have to be adjusted, depending on the size of the people in the chosen photo.) Coat the backs of the hats with the adhesive spray.

Place the hats on the photo, and press to adhere.

3. Use the tracing paper to make the arch template. (See Arch template on page 104.) From the gold patterned paper, make one arch. Use the fine paintbrush to paint the title on the arch. Let dry. Coat the back of the arch with the adhesive spray. Referring to the photo for placement, set the arch approximately two-thirds of the way down from the top of the paper. Press in place.

4. Trim the small photo to 2³⁄₄" x 2³⁄₄" (7 cm x 7 cm). Place the photo 3" (7.5 cm) from the right edge and flush with the bottom edge of the brown paper. Use the pencil to mark the brown paper at the corners for placement. Coat the back of the photo with adhesive spray. Press in place.

5. Grip one end of the red wire with the needle-nose pliers, and make a coil ³⁄₄" (2 cm) in diameter. Remove the pliers, and using the spoon template as a guide, continue shaping the wire into a spoon. (See template on page 105.) Cut the end of the wire with the wire cutters. Make two more spoons. From the blue wire, cut one 2" (5 cm) length. Twist the blue wire three times around the neck of one of the red spoons. Use the wire cutters to trim the ends of the wire. Use the pliers to fold the ends in. Repeat for the remaining spoons.

6. From the double-sided adhesive sheet, cut six to nine ¹⁄₁₆" x 1" (0.2 cm x 2.5 cm) strips. Peel off the protective paper, and, following the contours of the red wire, carefully attach the strips to the backsides of the spoons. Remove the remaining protective paper from the strips. Referring to the photo for placement, set the spoons on the brown paper. Press to adhere.

7. Use the kneaded rubber eraser to remove all pencil marks.

Favorite Books

This fine-gauge wire does double duty: it illustrates a love of reading, and it binds the paper books together.

Materials

- photo
- one 12" x 12" (30.5 cm x 30.5 cm) sheet wheat paper
- one 8 1/2" x 11" (21.5 cm x 28 cm) sheet white paper
- one 8 1/2" x 11" (21.5 cm x 28 cm) sheet cream paper
- one 8 1/2" x 11" (21.5 cm x 28 cm) sheet light peach paper
- archival-quality adhesive spray
- yellow 24-gauge coated wire
- double-sided adhesive sheet, such as Peel-N-Stick
- brown pencil
- self-adhesive foam spacers

Tools

- craft knife
- metal-edged ruler
- pencil
- 1/8" (0.3 cm) round paper punch
- needle-nose pliers
- wire cutters
- black fine-tip marker

Instructions

1. Using the ruler and knife, trim the peach paper to 8 1/2" x 7 3/4" (21.5 cm x 20 cm). Trim the photo to 4 7/8" x 6 5/8" (12.5 cm x 17 cm). Place the photo 1/2" (1 cm) from the left edge and 1/4" (0.6 cm) from the bottom edge of the peach paper. Mark the peach paper at the corners for placement. Coat the back of the photo with the adhesive spray. Press in place. Use the marker to print the title on the white paper (or do this on a computer). Center the title, and trim the white paper to 1 3/4" x 3 1/4" (4.5 cm x 8.5 cm). Coat the back with adhesive spray. Referring to the photo for placement, press the title box in place next to the photo.

2. Place the peach paper 1 3/4" (4.5 cm) from the left edge, flush with the top edge of the wheat paper. Mark the wheat paper at the corners for placement. Coat the back of the peach paper with adhesive spray. Press in place.

3. Cut one 10" (25.5 cm) length of the wire. Grip one end of the wire with the pliers, and make a coil 1/2" (1 cm) in diameter. Remove the pliers. Using the heart template as a guide, shape the wire into a heart. (See Small Heart template on page 102.) After forming the bottom half of the

heart, grip the opposite end of the wire and make a second coil to complete the shape. Cut the end of the wire with the wire cutters. Referring to the photo for placement, set the heart on the peach paper. From the double-sided adhesive sheet, cut one 3/16" x 2 1/2" (0.2 cm x 6.5 cm) strip. Peel off the protective paper, and attach the strip to a larger strip of peach paper. Trim the paper to match the adhesive. Cut the strip into thirds. Remove the remaining protective paper, and secure it to the paper with adhesive strip.

4. From the cream paper, cut three 2 1/4" x 2 3/4" (6 cm x 7 cm) rectangles. Using the brown pencil, write one book title on each rectangle. From the white paper, cut three 2 1/4" x 2 3/4" (6 cm x 7 cm) rectangles. Place one cream rectangle on one white rectangle. Referring to Diagram A, offset the rectangles. Using the hole punch, punch seven holes through both layers of the paper, 1/4" (0.6 cm) from the left edge of the cream rectangle. Remove the protective paper from the foam spacers, and attach one spacer on each corner of the white rectangle. Align the punched holes; attach the cream rectangle to the white rectangle. Repeat for the remaining books. From the yellow wire, cut three 10"

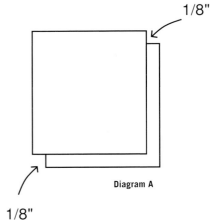

1/8"

Diagram A

1/8"

(25.5 cm) lengths. Wrap one length around the pencil eight times to create a spiral. Remove the pencil. Thread the spiraled wire through both sets of holes of one book. Using the wire cutters, trim the ends. Use the pliers to bend the ends toward the spiral. Place the book on the work surface, and carefully flatten the wire spiral. Repeat with the remaining books.

5. Place one book 1 3/4" (4.5 cm) from the left edge and 3/4" (2 cm) from the bottom edge of the wheat paper. Align horizontally. Place the remaining books on the wheat paper, allowing 5/8" (1.5 cm) between each book. Mark the wheat paper at the corners for placement. Coat the backs with adhesive spray. Press in place. Use the eraser to remove pencil marks.

Quilling

This art form got its name from 14th-century artists who rolled paper strips on the end of a quill to curl them. These lacy papers were then used to decorate Bible pages. Coiled papers can be shaped through pinching and folding into all sorts of recognizable images, such as people, snowflakes, and insects. Quilling is also called paper filigree.

The following instructions call for a quilling tool. A quilling tool is a short metal rod with a narrow tip. The tip is split to accommodate the end of the paper strip. If a quilling tool is not available, the paper strips can be coiled onto a toothpick or a hat pin. The quilling tool, however, creates a more uniform coil because the end of the paper strip is held securely in its tip.

Sample 1. Adhere fanciful curls to the top of a window frame to make a perfect focal point for a Victorian house.

Sample 2. Add pizzazz to a flat tag with crazy-quilled curlicues.

Sample 3. Create swirling, quilled snowflakes to cover a simple snowman silhouette.

Flower Girls

Little girls sporting curly hair and frilly dresses are fixtures at weddings and summer parties. In fact, these tresses look as if they were curled with a bird quill. Coiled paper flowers are the perfect complement to this angelic photo.

Materials

- photo
- one 12" x 12" (30.5 cm x 30.5 cm) sheet cream paper
- one 8 1/2" x 11" (21.5 cm x 28 cm) sheet pink patterned paper
- one 8 1/2" x 11" (21.5 cm x 28 cm) sheet light green patterned paper
- pink quilling paper
- green quilling paper
- white craft glue
- brown pencil
- brown acrylic paint
- archival-quality adhesive spray

Tools

- metal-edged ruler
- craft knife
- pencil
- quilling tool
- scissors
- toothpick
- flat paintbrush, 3/4" (2 cm) wide
- paper towel
- kneaded rubber eraser

Instructions

1. Using the ruler and knife, trim the pink patterned paper to 7 3/4" x 11" (20 cm x 28 cm). Place the pink paper 1" (2.5 cm) from the left edge and 1/2" (1 cm) from the top edge of the cream paper. Use the pencil to lightly mark the cream paper at the corners of the pink paper for placement. Following the manufacturer's directions, coat the back of the pink paper with the adhesive spray. Press in place. Trim the photo to 5" x 7" (12.5 cm x 18 cm). Place the photo 2 3/4" (7 cm) from the left edge and 1 3/4" (4.5 cm) from the top edge of the cream paper. Use the pencil to mark the pink paper at the corners of the photo for placement. Coat the back of the photo with adhesive spray. Press in place.

2. From the pink quilling paper, cut one 4" (10 cm) length. Insert one end of the paper into the quilling tool, and coil the paper to make a flower. Remove the curled paper from the tool. Repeat to make 11

more flowers. From the green quilling paper, cut one 6" (15 cm) length. Fold the strip in half lengthwise. Insert one end into the quilling tool, and coil the paper to within 1/2" (1 cm) of the fold to make a leaf. Insert the other end in the quilling tool and coil the paper to within 1/2" (1 cm) of the fold to make a second leaf. Use the toothpick to apply a small amount of craft glue, 1/2" (1 cm) from one side of the fold. Press the leaves together to make a stem. Repeat to make 11 more stems with leaves.

3. From the green paper, cut three 3 1/8" (8 cm) squares. Overlapping the pink paper, place one square 1/4" (0.6 cm) from the right edge and 3/4" (2 cm) from the top edge of the cream paper. Allowing 3/8" (1.5 cm) between squares, place the remaining two squares below the top square. Use the pencil to mark the pink and cream papers at the corners of the

squares for placement. Coat the backs of the squares with adhesive spray. Press them in place to adhere. Use the toothpick to apply a small amount of craft glue to the back of one flower. Referring to the photo for placement, press the flower in place in the top-left corner of the top square. Apply a small amount of glue to the back of one stem with leaves. Press in place below the flower. Repeat to attach remaining flowers and stems with leaves.

4. Use the brown pencil to write the title. Dilute the brown acrylic paint to approximately three parts water to one part paint. Using two continuous, horizontal strokes, paint over the title. Blot the paint with a paper towel, if necessary.

5. Use the kneaded rubber eraser to remove all pencil marks.

Live, Laugh, Love

These quilled papers look great on the stamped-wallpaper background. The simple title prompts further inspection of the candid and light-hearted photos.

Materials

- One 12" x 12" (30.5 cm x 30.5 cm) sheet ivory paper
- three floral stamps, with image size $1^1/_2$" (4 cm) to 3" (7.5 cm)
- pink ink
- brown acrylic paint
- white quilling paper
- white craft glue
- archival-quality adhesive spray

Tools

- tracing paper
- pencil
- metal-edged ruler
- craft knife
- quilling tool
- scissors
- toothpick
- round-tip liner brush
- kneaded rubber eraser

Instructions

1. Lay the tracing paper over the bottom 5" (12.5 cm) of the ivory paper. Using the stamps and the ink, stamp the top 7" (18 cm) of the ivory paper in a random pattern. Let dry.

2. Use the pencil to mark light horizontal lines at 2" (5 cm), $4^1/_4$" (11 cm), and $6^1/_2$" (16.5 cm) from the top edge of the ivory paper. Paint the title on the marked lines using the round-tip liner brush and brown acrylic paint. Let dry. Use the kneaded rubber eraser to remove the pencil lines. Mark a second set of horizontal lines with the pencil at $2^1/_4$" (6 cm), $4^1/_2$" (11.5 cm), and $6^3/_4$" (17 cm) from the top edge of the cream paper.

3. From the quilling paper, cut one 8" (20.5 cm) length. Insert one end of the paper in the quilling tool, and coil 4" (10 cm) of the paper. Remove the paper from the tool. Insert the opposite end of the paper in the quilling tool, and coil the remaining 4" (10 cm) in the opposite direction to make an "S" shape. Repeat to make 23 more "S" shapes. Use the toothpick to apply a small amount of craft glue to the back of one "S" shape. Referring to the photo for placement and using the top pencil line as a guide, press the "S" shape in place. Repeat, gluing a total of 8 "S" shapes per line. Let dry.

4. Using the ruler and knife, trim the photos to the following sizes, from left to right: $2^5/_8$" x $2^3/_4$" (6.5 cm x 7 cm), $3^3/_8$" x $2^3/_4$" (8.5 cm x 7 cm), and $3^1/_8$" x $2^3/_4$" (8 cm x 7 cm). Place the left photo 1" (2.5 cm) from the left edge and 1" (2.5 cm) from the bottom edge of the ivory paper. Aligning the top and bottom edges and allowing $3/_8$" (1 cm) between the photos, place the remaining two photos on the ivory paper. Use the pencil to mark the ivory paper at the corners of the photos for placement. Coat the backs of the photos with adhesive spray. Press in place.

5. With the kneaded rubber eraser, remove all pencil marks.

Pencil Shadowing

This treatment was adapted from charcoal rubbing, an activity of genealogists and curiosity seekers. For charcoal rubbing, a sheet of blank paper is placed on a tombstone or a monument and then rubbed with charcoal. The stone's or monument's texture and design are transferred to the paper. Other soft mediums, such as colored pencils, chalk, and pastel sticks, also create designs when rubbed on raised textures. The patterns made with colored pencils are subtle and nonsmearing. Those made with chalk and pastel sticks are more dramatic because there is greater contrast between the dark and the light values. Paper rubbed with chalk and pastel sticks should be sprayed with fixative before being placed in an album.

Sample 1. Rub a pencil over nine round-top buttons. Then rub the paper on corrugated paper. Rotate and repeat to make a border design.

Sample 2. Rub the pencil over a needlepoint canvas to make this texture. The design can be used to suggest a screen door or a lacy tablecloth.

Sample 3. Rub the surface of corrugated paper to create the waves; a sticker floats in the foreground.

Leaf Shadows

This treatment provides a quick and subtle way to enhance solid paper. It also enables your hole punches to do double duty.

Materials

- photo
- one 12" x 12" (30.5 cm x 30.5 cm) sheet sage paper
- one 8 1/2" x 11" (21.5 cm x 28 cm) sheet taupe paper
- one 8 1/2" x 11" (21.5 cm x 28 cm) sheet handmade paper with embedded leaves
- one 8 1/2" x 11" (21.5 cm x 28 cm) sheet pink vellum
- scrap of cardstock (any color)
- printed announcement
- black photo corners
- archival-quality adhesive spray
- taupe pencil

Tools

- leaf punch
- craft knife
- metal-edged ruler
- pencil
- tracing paper
- scissors
- kneaded rubber eraser
- black fine-tip marker (optional)

Instructions

1. Use the leaf punch to punch a leaf shape in the cardstock. Place the vellum on the punched card stock. Using the flat side of the taupe pencil's tip, gently color over the punched-out leaf to create a leaf image. Move the cardstock around, repeat to make 10 more leaves along the right edge of the vellum. Referring to the photo for placement, punch two leaf shapes on the right side of vellum. Place the vellum sheet 5/8" (1.5 cm) from the right edge and 3/8" (1 cm) from the top edge of the sage paper. Use the pencil to lightly mark the sage paper at the corners of the vellum for placement. Following the manufacturer's directions, coat the back of the vellum with adhesive spray. Press in place.

2. Referring to the photo for placement, punch three leaf shapes on the left side and the bottom of the handmade paper. Place the handmade paper 2 1/2" (6.5 cm) from the right edge and 5/8" (1.5 cm) from the top edge of the sage paper. Use the

pencil to mark the pink vellum and the sage paper at the corners of the handmade paper for placement. Coat the back of the handmade paper with adhesive spray. Press in place.

3. Using the ruler and knife, trim the photo to 4 1/4" x 5 1/2" (11 cm x 14 cm). Place the photo 3 1/2" (9 cm) from the right edge and 1 1/4" (4 cm) from the top edge of the sage paper. Use the pencil to mark the handmade paper at the corners of the photo for placement. Following the manufacturer's directions, attach the photo to the handmade paper with the photo corners.

4. With the text centered, use the knife to trim the announcement to 4 1/4" x 2 1/2" (11 cm x 6.5 cm). Place the announcement 3" (7.5 cm) from the right edge, and 2 3/8" (6 cm) from the bottom edge of the sage paper. Use the pencil to mark the handmade paper at the corners of the announcement for placement. Coat the

back of the announcement with adhesive spray. Press in place.

5. Use the tracing paper to make the leaf template. From the taupe paper, cut one leaf shape. Coat the back of the leaf shape with adhesive spray. Refer to the photo for placement. Press the leaf shape on the handmade paper, overlapping the announcement.

6. Use the kneaded rubber eraser to erase all pencil marks.

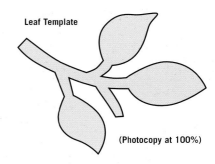

Leaf Template

(Photocopy at 100%)

Travel Textures

Collecting items to feature is as much fun as revealing the patterns. Group small items such as buttons, and overlap flat items such as coins.

Materials

- photos
- one 12" x 12" (30.5 cm x 30.5 cm) sheet brown paper
- one 8 $\frac{1}{2}$" x 11" (21.5 cm x 28 cm) sheet black paper
- one 8 $\frac{1}{2}$" x 11" (21.5 cm x 28 cm) sheet yellow paper
- one 8 $\frac{1}{2}$" x 11" (21.5 cm x 28 cm) sheet corrugated paper (any color)
- embossed tin
- white pencil
- archival-quality adhesive spray

Tools

- 3-D items with articulated textures, such as keys, coins, jewelry, and silverware
- craft knife
- metal-edged ruler
- pencil
- kneaded rubber eraser
- black fine-tip marker (optional)

Instructions

1. Place the three-dimensional items on the work surface. Place the black paper over the items. Use the flat side of the tip of the white pencil, and gently color over the raised surfaces of the items to create the images. After reproducing the desired number of images, fill in the negative spaces by repeating the process over the corrugated paper and the tin. Using the ruler and the knife, trim the decorated paper to 6 $\frac{1}{4}$" x 5 $\frac{1}{2}$" (16 cm x 14 cm). Following the manufacturer's directions, coat the back of the black paper with adhesive spray. Press the paper in the top-right corner of the brown paper to adhere.

2. Using the ruler and knife, trim the photos to the following sizes, clockwise from left: 5 $\frac{1}{8}$" x 5 $\frac{1}{8}$" (13 cm x 13 cm), 2 $\frac{1}{4}$" x 2 $\frac{1}{4}$" (6 cm x 6 cm), 5 $\frac{1}{2}$" x 6 $\frac{1}{2}$" (14 cm x 16.5 cm), and 4 $\frac{1}{2}$" x 5 $\frac{1}{4}$" (11.5 cm x 13.5 cm). Referring to the photo for placement, arrange the large photos on the brown paper. Place the top-right photo 3" (7.5 cm) from the right edge and $\frac{1}{4}$" (0.6 cm) from the top edge of the black paper. Use the pencil to lightly mark the brown paper and the black paper at the corners of the photos for placement. Coat the backs of the photos with adhesive spray. Press the photos in place.

3. Use the marker to print the title on the yellow paper (or do this on a computer). With the title centered, trim the paper to 4" x 1" (10 cm x 2.5 cm). Coat the back of the title box with adhesive spray. Referring to the photo for placement, press the title box along the bottom edge of the black paper.

4. Use the kneaded rubber eraser to remove all pencil marks.

Eyelets

Eyelets are small embellishments that pack a big punch. They not only are intrinsically attractive but also enable you to attach die-cuts to a page and layer paper without using adhesives. You can use them to reinforce holes from which you can hang, connect, or attach 3-D accents. They are available in a wide variety of sizes, colors, and shapes—literally from A to Z: alligators to zinnias. The tools required to inset eyelets are a hole punch (match the diameter of the punch with the diameter of the eyelets), an eyelet setter, and a hammer. Be sure to work on a cutting mat or other protective surface.

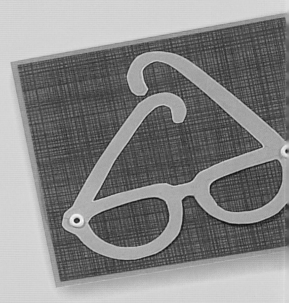

Sample 2. Use eyelets for decoration only. Eyelet hinges add flash to a pair of paper sunglasses.

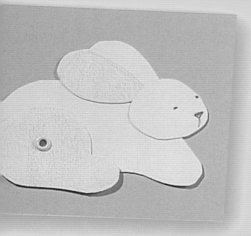

Sample 1. Make the hind leg of this rabbit movable by using an eyelet that acts as a joint.

Sample 3. Use eyelets and laces to add realism to an ordinary work boot.

Make Believe

This page highlights the versatility of eyelets. They are used to suspend swingy strands of beads and also to hold a vellum screen in place over a dreamy butterfly.

Materials

- one 12" x 12" (30.5 cm x 30.5 cm) sheet white paper
- one 12" x 12" (30.5 cm x 30.5 cm) sheet turquoise patterned paper
- one 8½" x 11" (21.5 cm x 28 cm) sheet purple paper
- one 8½" x 11" (21.5 cm x 28 cm) sheet pink paper
- one 8½" x 11" (21.5 cm x 28 cm) sheet cream paper
- one 8½" x 11" (21.5 cm x 28 cm) sheet violet paper
- one 8½" x 11" (21.5 cm x 28 cm) sheet white vellum
- one 8½" x 11" (21.5 cm x 28 cm) sheet white-and-yellow stripe paper
- one 8½" x 11" (21.5 cm x 28 cm) sheet green patterned paper
- one 8" (20.5 cm) green border sticker
- purple eyelets
- peach eyelets
- white thread
- assorted seed and bugle beads: gold, silver, opaque white, and clear
- archival-quality adhesive spray
- archival-quality tape
- double-sided adhesive sheet, such as Peel-N-Stick

Tools

- tracing paper
- metal-edged ruler
- craft knife
- scissors
- pencil
- beading needle
- hole punch
- eyelet setter
- hammer
- kneaded rubber eraser
- black fine-tip marker (optional)

Instructions

1. Using the ruler and knife, trim the turquoise paper to an 11½" x 11½" (29 cm x 29 cm) square. Coat the back with adhesive spray. Center on the white paper, and press in place.

2. Use the tracing paper to make the templates for the feather and the mask. (See Feather template on page 104 and Mask template on page 105.) Referring to the photo, cut the shapes from the corresponding colors. Tape the pink trim piece to the back of the purple mask piece. From the double-sided adhesive sheet, cut ⅛" (0.3 cm)-wide strips. Trim the strips to fit the back of the feather. Peel off the protective paper, and attach the adhesive shape to the back of the feather. Remove the remaining protective paper, and press the feather in place on the mask.

3. Punch holes on the mask where indicated. Inset the purple eyelets in the holes. Using the needle, string one gold bead on the thread. Tie the end of the thread around the bead to secure. Continue threading to make a 1½" (4 cm) strand. Insert the opposite end of thread through the left eyelet, and use the tape to secure the thread to the back of the mask. Trim the thread.

Repeat for the remaining eyelets. Note: Center strands measure 1¾" (4.5 cm).

4. Attach the border sticker 1½" (4 cm) from the left edge and 2" (5 cm) from the top edge of the white paper. Place the mask 1¼" (4 cm) from the left edge and ¼" (0.6 cm) from the top edge of the white paper. Mark the turquoise paper at the top and the bottom for placement. Coat the back with adhesive spray. Press in place.

5. Use the tracing paper to make the templates for the butterfly. (See Butterfly template on page 104.) Referring to the photo, cut the shapes from the corresponding colors. Coat the back of the pink wings with adhesive spray. Center and press to adhere the cream wings. From the double-sided adhesive sheet, cut one ⅛" x 1" (0.3 cm x 2.5 cm) strip. Peel off the protective paper, and attach the adhesive to the back of the body. Remove the remaining protective paper, and attach the body to the wings. Place the butterfly 1⅜" (3.5 cm) from the right edge and 1¼" (4 cm) from the bottom edge of the white paper. Mark the turquoise paper for placement. Coat the back of the butterfly with adhesive spray. Press in place. Use the eraser to remove pencil marks.

6. From the white vellum, cut one 3⅜" x 3⅜" (8.5 cm x 8.5 cm) square. Center and place the square over the butterfly. Use the hole punch to punch holes through all the layers, at each corner of the vellum. Using the eyelet setter and hammer, inset the peach eyelets in the holes.

7. Trim the photo to a 5" x 5" (12.5 cm x 12.5 cm) square. Place the photo 2¼" (6 cm) from the left edge and ⅞" (2 cm) from the bottom edge of the white paper. Mark the turquoise paper for placement. Coat the back with adhesive spray. Press in place. From the white-and-yellow striped paper, cut one 4½" x 1½" (11 cm x 4 cm) rectangle. Coat the back with adhesive spray. Referring to the photo for placement, press in place, with the top edge ¼" (0.6 cm) above the top edge of the photo. Use the marker to print the title on the green patterned paper (or do this on a computer). Trim the title box to 5" x ⅞" (12.5 cm x 2 cm). Coat the back with adhesive spray. Referring to the photo for placement, press in place.

8. Use the eraser to remove pencil marks.

Winter Wind

Eyelets help suspend these ornamental tags so that they can move back and forth according to the weather.

Materials

- photo
- one 12" x 12" (30.5 cm x 30.5 cm) sheet black paper
- one 8½" x 11" (21.5 cm x 28 cm) sheet wheat paper
- one 8½" x 11" (21.5 cm x 28 cm) sheet white paper
- two 2" x 3" (5 cm x 7.5 cm) tags with string
- one 1½" x 2" (4 cm x 5 cm) tag with string
- peach eyelets
- snowflake eyelets
- white milky pen
- archival-quality adhesive spray
- archival-quality tape
- double-sided adhesive sheet, such as Peel-N-Stick

Tools

- tracing paper
- metal-edged ruler
- craft knife
- scissors
- pencil
- hole punch
- eyelet setter
- hammer
- kneaded rubber eraser
- black fine-tip marker (optional)

Instructions

1. Use the tracing paper to make the templates for the wind. (See Wind template on page 103.) From the cream paper, cut the wind shapes. Following the manufacturer's directions, coat the backs of the wind pieces with adhesive spray. Press the pieces in the top-right corner of the black paper to adhere.

2. On the white paper, use the marker to print the letters for "winter" in various sizes and styles (or do this on a computer using various fonts). Using the scissors, cut each letter from the white paper. From the double-sided adhesive sheet, cut one ¼" x 3" (0.6 cm x 7.5 cm) strip. Trim the strip to fit the backs of the letters. Peel off the protective paper, and attach the adhesive sheet to the backs of the letters. Remove the remaining protective paper, and press the letters in place on the tags.

Use the hole punch to punch holes in the black paper at 3⅞" (10 cm) from the left edge and 1⅜" (3.5 cm) from the top edge, and at 6" (15 cm) from the left edge and 2" (5 cm) from the top edge. Punch a hole in the wind where indicated. Following the manufacturer's directions, inset the peach eyelets in the holes. Thread the tag strings through the corresponding eyelets. Use the archival-quality tape to secure the strings to the back of the black paper. Trim ends. Arrange the tags at the desired angle. Use the pencil to lightly mark the black paper at the corners of the tags for placement. From the double-sided adhesive sheet, cut three ¾" (2 cm) squares. Peel off the protective paper, and attach the adhesive to the backs of the tags. Remove the remaining protective paper, and press the tags in place to adhere.

3. Using the ruler and pencil, mark a line of five horizontal dots 1⅝" (4 cm) from the bottom edge of the black paper and spaced 1⅞" (5 cm) apart. Use the hole punch to punch holes over the dots. Use the eyelet setter and hammer to inset the snowflake eyelets in the holes.

4. Using the ruler and knife, trim the photo to 5" x 3½" (12.5 cm x 9 cm). Place the photo on the black paper 3" (7.5 cm) from the left edge and 2¾" (7 cm) from the bottom edge of the black paper. Use the pencil to mark the black paper at the corners of the photo for placement. Coat the back of the photo with adhesive spray. Press in place.

5. Write the caption using the milky pen.

6. Use the kneaded rubber eraser to remove all pencil marks.

recipe
9
Sequins

Thumb through any clothing or home-decorating catalog, and you will see '60s fashion reborn, complete with exotic '60s embellishments, including glistening sequins. A few well-placed sequins can add sizzle and sophistication to a page layout because the shiny surface of the sequins provides the perfect complement to the matte finish of the paper. Placing sequins on a page creates a shimmering surface texture that resembles water or snow. Sequins come in all shapes and sizes and can be glued or stitched to the paper. You can also stitch them to a separate swatch of fabric, which you can then glue to the paper.

Sample 1. Combine $^2/_5$" (1 cm) sequins with twisted wire for this attractive trim.

Sample 2. Alternate $^1/_5$" (0.2 cm) sequins and tiny beads on a wire wreath for a charming baby accent.

Sample 3. Surround novelty snowflake sequins with ultra-thin gold wire, which is embedded in the dark teal fabric.

Vegas Vacation

These pastel sequins bring to mind both neon lights and celestial stars.
They serve as the perfect finishing touch for a well-dressed page.

Materials

- photo
- one 12" x 12" (30.5 cm x 30.5 cm) sheet purple paper
- one 8½" x 11" (21.5 cm x 28 cm) glossy blue paper
- one 8½" x 11" (21.5 cm x 28 cm) glossy yellow paper
- one flat postcard
- one folded postcard
- ⅕" (0.2 cm) sequins in assorted colors
- pastel beads, size 10/0
- light blue thread
- archival-quality adhesive spray
- archival-quality tape
- white milky pen

Tools

- craft knife
- metal-edged ruler
- pencil
- needle
- scissors
- kneaded rubber eraser

Instructions

1. Using the ruler and knife, trim the flat postcard to 5¼" x 4⅜" (13.5 cm x 11 cm). Place several sequins on the postcard. Use the pencil to mark the chosen points for the sequins. Thread the needle, and insert the needle from the back of the postcard at one of the marked points. Working from back to front, thread one sequin on the needle. Then thread one bead on the needle. Reinsert the needle through the top of the sequin and down through the postcard. Repeating this process, stitch the remaining sequins and beads to the postcard at the marked points. Use the archival-quality tape to secure the ends of the thread to the back of the postcard. Trim ends.

2. Place the postcard ⅜" (1 cm) from the right edge and ⅜" (1 cm) from the top edge of the purple paper. Use the pencil to mark the purple paper at the corners of the postcard for placement. Following the manufacturer's directions, coat the back of the postcard with adhesive spray. Press in place.

3. Place the folded postcard 1⅜" (3.5 cm) from the left edge and 2" (5 cm) from the top edge of the purple paper. Use the pencil to mark the purple paper at the corners of the postcard for placement. Coat the back of the postcard with adhesive spray. Press in place.

4. Trim the photo to 5½" x 4" (14 cm x 10 cm). Overlapping the bottom inside corner of the folded postcard, place the photo 2¾" (7 cm) from the right edge and 2¼" (6 cm) from the bottom edge of the purple paper. Use the pencil to mark the purple paper at the corners of the photo for placement. Coat the back of the photo with adhesive spray. Press in place.

5. Cut one 5¼" x ⅝" (13.5 cm x 1.5 cm) strip from the blue paper. Center the strip, and use the pencil to mark nine dots ½" (1 cm) apart on the strip. Referring to Diagram A, stitch the sequins and the beads on the strip. Place the strip 1¼" (4 cm) from the left edge and 1" (2.5 cm) from the bottom edge of the purple paper. Use the pencil to mark the purple paper at the corners of the postcard for placement. Coat the back of the strip with adhesive spray. Press in place.

6. Cut one 4" x ⅜" (10 cm x 1 cm) strip from the yellow paper. Coat the back of the strip with adhesive spray. Center and place the yellow strip beneath the blue strip. Press to adhere.

7. Write the caption using the milky pen.

8. Use the kneaded rubber eraser to remove all pencil marks.

Wishing For

The ripples created by a tossed penny extend beyond this photo, thanks to five meandering strands of sequins. The white sequins represent both light and movement.

I am
wishing
for :
skates
a puppy
sunny days
and
more pennies

Materials

- photo
- one 12" x 12" (30.5 cm x 30.5 cm) sheet blue patterned paper
- one 12" x 12" (30.5 cm x 30.5 cm) sheet white vellum
- one 8½" x 11" (21.5 cm x 28 cm) sheet pink vellum
- three paper pennies
- 1½" (4 cm) white sequins
- white thread
- archival-quality adhesive spray
- double-sided adhesive sheet, such as Peel-N-Stick
- black pencil

Tools

- craft knife
- metal-edged ruler
- pencil
- needle
- scissors
- white craft glue
- toothpick
- kneaded rubber eraser
- black fine-tip marker (optional)

Instructions

1. Using the ruler and the knife, trim the photo to 6" x 4½" (15 cm x 11.5 cm). Place the photo 1⅝" (4 cm) from the left edge and 1¾" (4.5 cm) from the top edge of the white vellum. Use the pencil to lightly mark the white vellum at the corners of the photo for placement. Referring to the photo for placement, set the paper pennies on the white vellum. Use the pencil to mark the placement for the center of each penny. With the craft knife, cut circles 1" (2.5 cm) in diameter around each mark.

2. Following the manufacturer's directions, coat the back of the white vellum with adhesive spray. Place the vellum on the blue patterned paper, and press to adhere. Coat the back of the photo with adhesive spray. Press in place. From the double-sided adhesive sheet, cut three circles, ¾" (2 cm) in diameter. Peel off the protective paper, and attach the adhesive sheet to the backs of the pennies. Remove the remaining protective paper, and press the pennies in place inside the circles.

3. Use the marker to print the title on the pink vellum (or do this on a computer). Trim the pink vellum to 3" x 2" (7.5 cm x 5 cm). Place the title box ½" (1 cm) from the right edge and 3¾" (9.5 cm) from the bottom edge of the white vellum. Use the pencil to mark the white vellum at the corners of the title box for placement. From the double-sided adhesive sheet, cut four small triangles. Peel off the protective paper, and attach the triangles to the corners of the message box. Remove the remaining protective paper, and press in place.

4. Use the black pencil to write the captions below the title box.

5. Cut one 20" (51 cm) length of thread, and insert the thread in the needle. String a sequin on the thread, and choose a point on the page at which to begin a sequin strand. Use the toothpick to apply a small dot of white glue on the white vellum. Place the first sequin, convex side down, on the glue, and hold it in place for a moment to secure. Working in small sections with three or four sequins at a time, continue stringing sequins on the thread and gluing them in place. Refer to the photo for spacing between sequins and for free-form shapes of strands. After completing one strand, trim the thread and repeat with four more strands. Completed strands are between 10" (25.5 cm) and 18" (45.5 cm) long.

6. Use the kneaded rubber eraser to remove all pencil marks.

Lace-Ups

Remember lace-up books? Generations of children were kept quiet on car trips, in waiting rooms, and in church services by drawing colored shoelaces through holes in chunky storybooks. The accents in these projects are punched with a small hole punch so that the component parts can be layered and laced together. Most hole punches don't reach to the interior of the page, so borders are a natural area for incorporating this technique. Relive your youth and, at the same time, add interest to your compositions. Try lacing with additional soft materials, such as yarn, twine, or bias-cut fabric strips. You can also use fine wire, but regular wire is not recommended because it may tear the paper.

Sample 1. Lace up a paper basket with nubby twine.

Sample 2. Lace an edging onto a photo frame with soft ribbon.

Sample 3. Make a great page topper using a row of hearts connected with a strip of bias-cut fabric.

Desert Flowers

Re-create the drama of a desert flower with these graphic, lace-up flowers. The torn edges of the paper flowers resemble the ruffled edge of the real ones.

Materials

- photos
- one 12" x 12" (30.5 cm x 30.5 cm) sheet tan paper
- one 8 1/2" x 11" (21.5 cm x 28 cm) sheet tan patterned paper
- one 8 1/2" x 11" (21.5 cm x 28 cm) sheet dark pink paper
- one 8 1/2" x 11" (21.5 cm x 28 cm) sheet light pink paper
- 12" (30.5 cm) length cream plastic raffia
- archival-quality adhesive spray
- archival-quality tape
- black fine-tip marker

Tools

- craft knife
- metal-edged ruler
- pencil
- 1/8" (0.3 cm) round paper punch
- kneaded rubber eraser

Instructions

1. Using the ruler and the knife, cut one 1 3/8" x 9 1/4" (3.5 cm x 23.5 cm) strip from the tan patterned paper. From the dark pink paper, tear two flower shapes, 2" (5 cm) in diameter. Place one flower on the tan print strip, with the center of the flower at 1 3/8" (3.5 cm) from the bottom edge of the strip. Using the hole punch, punch four holes through both layers, approximately 1/2" (1 cm) apart. With the center of the flower at 4 1/4" (11 cm) from the bottom edge of the strip, place the remaining flower on the strip. Punch four holes through both layers. From the light pink paper, tear two circles for flower centers, 3/4" (2 cm) in diameter. Place one flower center on one flower. Working from the back to the front of the strip, thread the raffia up through one hole and down through the opposite diagonal hole. Repeat to create an X. Secure the ends of raffia to back of strip using the archival-quality tape. Repeat for the remaining flower.

2. Place the strip 5/8" (1.5 cm) from right edge and 1/4" (0.6 cm) from bottom edge of the tan paper. Use the pencil to lightly mark the tan paper at the corners of the strip for placement. Following the manufacturer's directions, coat the back of the strip with adhesive spray. Place in place.

3. Trim the photos to the following sizes, clockwise from left: 4" x 6" (10 cm x 15 cm), 3 1/4" x 5 1/2" (8.5 cm x 14 cm), and 5 3/4" x 4" (14.5 cm x 10 cm). Referring to the photo for placement, arrange the photos on the tan paper. Use the pencil to lightly mark the tan paper at the corners of the photos for placement. Coat the back of the photos with adhesive spray. Press in place.

4. Write the captions using the black marker.

5. Use the kneaded rubber eraser to remove all pencil marks.

Silver Celebration

A glitzy metallic-chenille stem is easily secured to this page with lacing. Because the chenille stem is sturdy enough to hold its shape, only a few stitches are needed.

Materials

- photo
- one 12" x 12" (30.5 cm x 30.5 cm) sheet blue paper
- one 8 1/2" x 11" (21.5 cm x 28 cm) sheet light blue paper
- one 8 1/2" x 11" (21.5 cm x 28 cm) sheet light gray paper
- one 12" (30.5 cm) silver metallic chenille stem
- 9" (23 cm) length gray embroidery floss
- letter stickers
- archival-quality adhesive spray
- archival-quality tape

Tools

- craft knife
- metal-edged ruler
- pencil
- 1/8" (0.3 cm) round paper punch
- wire cutter
- scissors
- kneaded rubber eraser

Instructions

1. Using the ruler and knife, trim the photo to 5" x 6 3/4" (12.5 cm x 17 cm). Following the manufacturer's directions, coat the back of the photo with adhesive spray. Place the photo on the gray paper, and press to adhere. Center the photo, and trim the gray paper to 5 1/4" x 7" (13.5 cm x 18 cm).

2. Trim the light blue paper to 8" x 9 1/2" (20.5 cm x 24 cm). Referring to Diagram A, punch six holes in the paper using the hole punch. Center the holes between the right and left edges of the paper and 3/4" (2 cm) from the bottom edge of the paper. Referring to Diagram B, bend the chenille stem. Use the wire cutter to trim the ends of chenille stem. Referring to Diagram C, place the shaped chenille stem on the paper. Working from back to front and from right to left, thread embroidery floss through the holes to secure chenille stem in place. Secure the ends of floss to back

of the paper using the archival-quality tape. Trim ends.

3. Referring to the photo for placement, place the mounted photo 3/8" (1 cm) from the top edge of the gray paper. Use the pencil to mark lightly the light blue paper at the corners of the mounted photo for placement. Coat the back of the gray paper with adhesive spray. Press in place.

4. Place the light blue paper on the blue paper 3/4" (2 cm) from the right edge and 3/8" (1 cm) from the top edge of the blue paper. Use the pencil to lightly mark the blue paper at the corners of the light blue paper for placement. Coat the back of the light blue paper with adhesive spray. Press in place.

5. Attach the stickers.

6. Use the kneaded rubber eraser to remove all pencil marks.

Diagram A

1 1/4" (3 cm)   7/16" (1 cm)

Diagram B

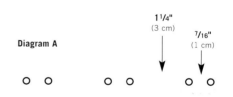

Diagram C

Weaving

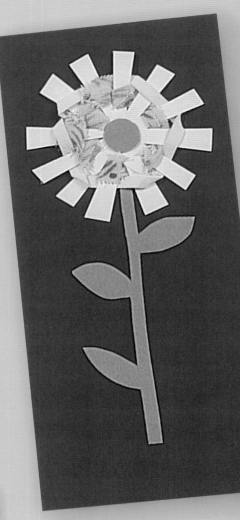

One kindergarten memory that we all share is weaving red and green paper strips to make a holiday place mat. Use this latent skill to create artistic page accents. Weaving is a straightforward technique, which can transform solid areas into intriguing patterns and configurations. For scrapbook layouts, use woven paper to make borders, shapes, backgrounds, and title boxes. It can naturally represent baskets, clothing, and rugs, and a simple tone-on-tone woven square looks great behind a journal message or a title box. Best of all, it is a great way to use your paper scraps.

Sample 1. After mastering the over-one-and-under-one weaving sequence, try weaving over one and under two.

Sample 2. Introduce floss or yarn into the weaving to add interest and change the texture.

Sample 3. Paper flower petals serve as spokes through which to weave. Weave in a circular pattern by starting in the center and working out.

Happy Birthday Heart

Meandering strands of yarn are worked into this expressive heart.

Materials

- photos
- one 12" x 12" (30.5 cm x 30.5 cm) sheet gold patterned paper
- one 8 1/2" x 11" (21.5 cm x 28 cm) sheet red patterned paper
- one 8 1/2" x 11" (21.5 cm x 28 cm) sheet black paper
- one 8 1/2" x 11" (21.5 cm x 28 cm) sheet tan paper
- one 8 1/2" x 11" (21.5 cm x 28 cm) sheet burgundy paper
- birthday card
- pink yarn
- letter stickers
- brown pencil
- archival-quality adhesive spray
- double-sided adhesive sheet, such as Peel-N-Stick

Tools

- craft knife
- scissors
- tracing paper
- metal-edged ruler
- pencil
- kneaded rubber eraser

Instructions

1. Place the birthday card 3 1/2" (9 cm) from the right edge and 3/8" (1 cm) from the bottom edge of the gold patterned paper. Use the pencil to lightly mark the gold paper at the corners of the card for placement. Following the manufacturer's directions, coat the back of the card with adhesive spray. Place the card on the gold paper, and press to adhere.

2. Using the ruler and knife, trim the photos to 2 1/2" x 3 1/2" (6.5 cm x 9 cm). Referring to the photo for placement, set the photos diagonally inside the card. Use the pencil to mark the gold paper at the corners of the photos for placement. Coat the backs of the photos with the adhesive spray. Place the photos inside the card, and press to adhere.

3. From the red patterned paper, tear two 1 1/2" x 11" (4 cm x 28 cm) strips. From the black paper, tear one 2" x 11" (5 cm x 28 cm) strip. Overlapping the left edge of gold paper, layer the strips on the left side of the gold paper. Coat the backs of the strips with adhesive spray. Place the strips on the gold paper, and press to adhere. Using the ruler and knife, trim the overlapping edges of the strips.

4. From the tan paper, cut one 4" x 4" (10 cm x 10 cm) square. Referring to Diagram A, cut 1/4" (0.6 cm)- to 3/8" (1 cm)-wide vertical strips to within 1/2" (1 cm) of the top of the square. From the burgundy paper, cut two 3" x 1/4" (7.5 cm x 0.6 cm) strips, and one 3" x 3/8" (7.5 cm x 1 cm) strip. From the pink yarn, cut two 8" (20.5 cm) lengths. Weave one narrow burgundy paper strip horizontally between strips of vertical tan paper. Weave one length of pink yarn horizontally between strips of brown paper. Note: Paper strips are woven with a basic over-under repeat. Yarn lengths are woven free-form, combining over-under repeats with loops that wrap completely around selected strips. Weave wide burgundy paper strip, followed by the remaining narrow burgundy paper strip, and finish with the remaining yarn length.

5. From the double-sided adhesive sheet, cut one 4" x 4" (10 cm x 10 cm) square. Peel off the protective paper, and attach the adhesive to the back of the woven heart. Use the tracing paper to make the heart template. (See Large Heart template on page 105.) Center and draw the heart on the front of the woven square. Cut the heart shape from the woven paper, but do not cut the ends of the yarn lengths or the ends of the paper strips. Referring to the photo for placement, remove the remaining protective paper, and attach the heart to the gold paper. Manipulate and arrange the ends of the yarn as desired. From the double-sided adhesive sheet, cut four 1/16" x 1/2" (0.2 cm x 1 cm) strips. Peel off the protective paper, and attach the adhesive sheet to the paper beneath the yarn ends. Remove the remaining protective paper, and press the yarn on the exposed adhesive. Trim the ends of the yarn and the ends of the paper strips, as desired.

6. Attach the stickers. Write the names and the date using the brown pencil.

7. Use the kneaded rubber eraser to remove all pencil marks.

Diagram A

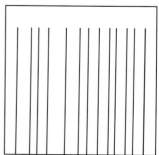

Moiré Border

Woven paper doesn't have to be confined to rigid right angles. Inserting curved strips into this border makes it flow.

Materials

- photo
- one 12" x 12" (30.5 cm x 30.5 cm) sheet dark brown paper
- one 12" x 12" (30.5 cm x 30.5 cm) sheet dark red paper
- one 8 1/2" x 11" (21.5 cm x 28 cm) sheet blue patterned paper
- one 8 1/2" x 11" (21.5 cm x 28 cm) sheet lavender paper
- one 8 1/2" x 11" (21.5 cm x 28 cm) sheet dark gray paper
- one 8 1/2" x 11" (21.5 cm x 28 cm) sheet light gray paper
- one 8 1/2" x 11" (21.5 cm x 28 cm) sheet blue paper
- one 8 1/2" x 11" (21.5 cm x 28 cm) sheet burgundy paper
- one 8 1/2" x 11" (21.5 cm x 28 cm) sheet black paper
- gold pencil
- archival-quality adhesive spray
- double-sided adhesive sheet, such as Peel-N-Stick

Tools

- craft knife
- tracing paper
- scissors
- metal-edged ruler
- pencil
- kneaded rubber eraser

Instructions

1. Using the ruler and knife, trim 1" (2.5 cm) from the top edge of the dark red paper. Following the manufacturer's directions, coat the back of the dark red paper. Exposing 1/2" (1 cm) on both the top and the bottom of the dark brown paper, attach the dark red paper to the dark brown paper. Press to adhere.

2. Using the ruler and knife, trim the photo to 4 3/4" x 7 5/8" (12 cm x 19.5 cm). Coat the back of the photo with the adhesive spray. Place the photo on the black paper, and press to adhere. Center the photo, and trim the black paper to 5 1/8" x 8" (13 cm x 20.5 cm). Place the mounted photo 1 1/4" (3 cm) from the top edge, and 1 3/4" (4.5 cm) from the left edge of the dark red paper. Use the pencil to lightly mark the dark red paper at the corners of the mounted photo for placement. Coat the back of the mounted photo with adhesive spray. Press in place.

3. Use the tracing paper to make the border template. (See Curvy Border template on page 105.) From the blue patterned paper, cut one border shape. Cut the curved strips to within 1/4" (0.6 cm) of the left edge of the border. From the following papers, cut curved strips of various lengths and widths: lavender, dark gray, light gray, blue, and burgundy. Weave the strips in an over-under pattern. Note: Experiment with the length of strips and the direction in which they are woven. To obtain a random and fluid look, taper the ends of some of the strips. Complete the weaving.

4. From the double-sided adhesive sheet, cut 5 1/2" x 11" (14 cm x 28 cm) rectangle. Peel off the protective paper, and attach the adhesive to the back of the woven border. Referring to the broken line on the border template, trim the long sides of the border. Remove the remaining protective paper, and attach the border on the right edge of the dark red paper.

5. Write the caption using the gold pencil.

6. Use the kneaded rubber eraser to remove all pencil marks.

Ribbon Embroidery

You don't need to confine embroidered silk flowers to the corner of a collar or the edge of a handkerchief. These delicate blooms make a lovely addition to a romantic scrapbook page. And don't be intimidated by the elegance and intricacy of silk ribbon embroidery. Even a novice embroiderer can create beautiful flowers and borders by mastering a few simple stitches. To achieve the desired fullness characteristic of this technique, practice the stitches on a paper scrap.

Sample 1. Determine the desired rose size, and, with the pencil, lightly draw a circle on the paper.

Sample 2. Use the needle and thread to make five spokes in the center of the marked circle. Tape the ends of the thread to the back of the paper to secure.

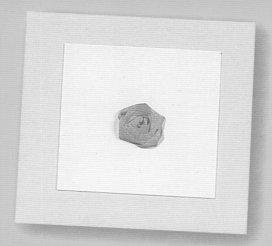

Sample 3. Bring the ribbon from the back of the paper through the center, and, working from the center out, weave the ribbon over and under the spokes. End by inserting the needle through the paper at the outer edge of the rose. Tape the ends of the ribbon to the back of the paper to secure.

Happy Birthday Window

Combine a running stitch and a Y stitch to create a playful border. The three-dimensional ribbon accent is as shiny as the dewy grass in the photo.

Materials

- photos
- one 12" x 12" (30.5 cm x 30.5 cm) sheet blue pinstripe paper
- one 8 1/2" x 11" (21.5 cm x 28 cm) sheet green patterned paper
- one 8 1/2" x 11" (21.5 cm x 28 cm) sheet emerald paper
- one 8 1/2" x 11" (21.5 cm x 28 cm) sheet yellow paper
- one 8 1/2" x 11" (21.5 cm x 28 cm) sheet mint patterned paper
- one 8 1/2" x 11" (21.5 cm x 28 cm) sheet blue paper
- archival-quality tape
- archival-quality adhesive spray
- double-sided adhesive sheet such as Peel-N-Stick
- 1/5" (0.2 cm) light green silk ribbon
- 1/5" (0.2 cm) lavender silk ribbon
- 5/8" (1.5 cm) blue paper blossoms

Tools

- scissors
- needle
- craft knife
- metal-edged ruler
- pencil
- kneaded rubber eraser
- black fine-tip marker (optional)

Instructions

1. Using the ruler and knife, trim the green patterned paper to a 7 7/8" x 7 7/8" (20 cm x 20 cm) square. Center and cut four 3" x 3" (7.5 cm x 7.5 cm) squares in the 7 7/8" x 7 7/8" (20 cm x 20 cm) square to make a mat. Use the marker to print the title on the blue paper. Center the title, and, using the ruler and knife, trim the blue paper to 3 1/2" x 3 1/2" (9 cm x 9 cm). Trim the emerald, yellow, and mint patterned papers to 3 1/2" x 3 1/2" (9 cm x 9 cm). Referring to the photo for placement, tape the papers to the back of the mat.

2. Cut the photos in circles 2 7/8" (7.5 cm) in diameter. Following the manufacturer's directions, coat the backs of the photos with adhesive spray. Center and press the photos in the centers of the three blank windows. Place the matted photos 1 1/4" (3 cm) from the right edge and 1 1/2" (4 cm) from the top edge of the pinstripe paper. Use the pencil to mark lightly the pinstripe paper at the corners of the mat for placement. Coat the back of the matted photos with adhesive spray. Press in place.

3. Using the ruler and the pencil, mark a line of 22 horizontal dots 5/8" (1.5 cm) below the bottom edge of the mat, and spaced 3/8" (1 cm) apart. Use the needle to slightly pierce the paper at each dot. Thread the needle with the light green ribbon. Insert the needle at the back of the paper through the far-right hole. Working right to left, stitch over-under (running stitch) through the paper at the pierced holes. Stitch loosely enough to create dimension with the ribbon. Use the archival-quality tape to secure the ends of the ribbon to the back of paper. Trim ends.

4. Refer to Diagram A for the Y stitch pattern. Mark the dots for the Y stitches between the running stitches. Using the needle, slightly pierce the paper at each dot. Bring the needle from the back to the front at A. Insert the needle at B. Pull the ribbon to the back until it forms a loose V shape. Bring the needle up at C and down at D to make a Y shape. Repeat to make four more Y stitches. Use the archival-quality tape to secure the ends of the ribbon to the back of the paper. Trim ends.

5. From the double-sided adhesive sheet, cut five circles, 3/8" (1 cm) in diameter. Peel off the protective paper, and attach the adhesive sheet to the backs of the blue blossoms. Remove the protective remaining paper, and attach the blossoms on the bottom of the mat.

6. Use the kneaded rubber eraser to remove all pencil marks.

Diagram A

Wedding Flowers

Special occasions call for special page treatments. Join the ribbon renaissance, and create exquisite roses of subtle color and rich texture to mark a special day.

Materials

- photo
- printed announcement
- one 12" x 12" (30.5 cm x 30.5 cm) sheet plum paper
- one 12" x 12" (30.5 cm x 30.5 cm) sheet gray patterned paper
- one 8¹⁄₂" x 11 (21.5 cm x 28 cm) sheet gray paper
- one 8¹⁄₂" x 11 (21.5 cm x 28 cm) sheet pink pearlescent paper
- ¹⁄₅" (0.2 cm) pink silk ribbon
- ¹⁄₅" (0.2 cm) mauve silk ribbon
- ¹⁄₅" (0.2 cm) olive silk ribbon
- pink thread
- archival-quality tape
- archival-quality adhesive spray

Tools

- scissors
- needle
- craft knife
- metal-edged ruler
- pencil
- kneaded rubber eraser

Instructions

1. Referring to Diagram A, lightly mark the top-right corner of the gray paper with a pencil for stitch placement. (See Stitch Placement diagram on page 102.) Using the needle, slightly pierce the paper at each dot. Referring to Diagram B for the spiderweb rose stitch, stitch three roses as indicated, using the pink ribbon. Use the needle and thread to make five spokes in the center of the marked circles. Use the archival-quality tape to secure the ends of the thread to the back of the paper. Bring the needle from the back to the front at the center of the circle. Referring to Diagram C, insert the needle through the front of the paper at the outer edge of the rose, and come up again at the center. Continue weaving the ribbon over and under each spoke until the rose is complete, stitching loosely enough to create dimension with the ribbon. Tape the ends of the ribbon to the back of the paper to secure. Trim ends. Stitch two roses, as indicated, using the mauve ribbon. Referring to Diagram D for the leaves and with olive ribbon, stitch the leaves as indicated. Bring the needle from the back to the front at A. Insert the needle through the center of the ribbon at B. Pull the ribbon to the back until it forms a point at B. Tape the ends of the ribbon to the back of the paper to secure. Trim ends.

2. Referring to the photo, place the gray patterned paper diagonally, with the top right corner 1¹⁄₄" (3 cm) from the right edge and 1¹⁄₄" (3 cm) from the top edge of the plum paper. Use the pencil to lightly mark the plum paper at the corner and the sides of the gray patterned paper for placement. Following the manufacturer's directions, coat the back of the gray patterned paper with adhesive spray. Press in place. Using the ruler and knife, trim the overlapping top, left, and bottom edges of gray patterned paper.

3. Referring to the photo above, place the gray paper diagonally on the gray patterned paper. Use the pencil to mark the gray patterned paper at the corners of the gray paper for placement. Coat the back of the gray paper with adhesive spray. Press in place. Trim the overlapping edge.

4. Trim the photo to 7" x 5" (18 cm x 12.5 cm). Place the photo diagonally on the gray paper. Use the pencil to mark the gray paper at the corners of the photo for placement. Coat the back of the photo with adhesive spray. Press in place. Trim the announcement to 6¹⁄₂" x 4¹⁄₂" (16.5 cm x 11.5 cm). Coat the back of the announcement with adhesive spray. Overlap 1¹⁄₄" (3 cm) of the bottom edge of the photo, and press in place to adhere.

From the pink pearlescent paper, cut one 3" x 2" x 2¹⁄₄" (7.5 cm x 5 cm x 5.5 cm) triangle. Coat the back of the triangle with the adhesive spray. Overlap the gray paper, and place the triangle in the top-right corner of the plum paper. Press to adhere.

5. Use the kneaded rubber eraser to erase all pencil marks.

Diagram B

Diagram C

Diagram D

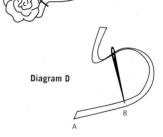

Shrink Plastic

Shrink plastic is made from plastic stock that is heated and stretched in two directions until a thin sheet is formed. This thin sheet can be decorated in a variety of ways. When it's heated again, the plastic returns to its original dimensions and overall thickness. It's a great material for creative scrapbook pages because the final product is sturdy but flat enough to integrate easily into a page layout. You can design the plastic sheet using a wide variety of art supplies, including stamping inks, paint, markers, pastel crayons, colored pencils, and metallic, rub-on highlighting products. You can also use scissors to trim and shape it and using ordinary paper punches to punch holes in it. Finished designs are then baked. The plastic shrinks to approximately 45 percent of its original size with a thickness of $1/16$" (0.2 cm). During the shrinking process, most art materials are permanently bonded to the surface. The shrinking process has a wonderful effect on the designs and colors that are applied before baking. Simple designs become crisper, elaborate designs look amazingly detailed, and colors appear rich and vibrant.

Sample 1. Begin to color a shrink-plastic tile with pencils before baking it.

Sample 2. Here is a finished shrink plastic tile featuring an orange background with purple dots.

Sample 3. Here, another color variation highlights the dot pattern theme.

Mother's Day Card

Use shrink plastic to create tiles that play off the motifs in a child's artwork. Use the tiles to create a colorful picture frame to house a photo of the artist.

Materials

- photo
- one 12" x 12" (30.5 cm x 30.5 cm) sheet dark brown paper
- two or three 9" x 12" (23 cm x 30.5 cm) sheets shrink plastic
- colored pencils, including white (Prisma Colors work best)
- double-sided adhesive sheet, such as Peel-N-Stick
- archival-quality adhesive spray

Tools

- craft knife
- metal-edged ruler
- pinking shears
- pencil
- kneaded rubber eraser

Instructions

1. Refer to the manufacturer's directions to calculate the desired size of shrink plastic after baking. Enlarge your designs accordingly. Using your chosen artwork as inspiration, trace or draw the designs on the rough side of the shrink plastic with a pencil. Color in the designs with the colored pencils. Using the ruler and knife, cut the squares that will surround the artwork from the plastic. Calculate the finished size for the frame. Use the pencil to trace the frame outline on the rough side of the shrink plastic, and color in the frame area with the colored pencils. Cut the window from the frame. Using the pinking shears, cut around the outside edge of the frame. Following the manufacturer's directions, bake the shrink plastic. Let cool.

2. Using the ruler and knife, trim the artwork, if necessary. Trim the photo to fit the finished plastic frame.

3. Place the artwork, the tiles, and the frame on the brown paper in your desired arrangement. Refer to the photo in the book for placement. Use the pencil to lightly mark the brown paper at the corners of the artwork, the tiles, and the frame. Following the manufacturer's directions, coat the backs of the artwork and the photo with adhesive spray. Press them in place to adhere. From the double-sided adhesive sheet, cut squares that are slightly smaller than the tiles. Peel off the protective paper, and attach the adhesive to the rough side of the tiles. Remove the remaining protective paper, and press the tiles in place to adhere.

4. From the double-sided adhesive sheet, cut strips slightly narrower than the finished frame. Peel off the protective paper, and attach the adhesive to the rough side of the frame. Trim the ends of the adhesive strips to fit. Remove the remaining protective paper, and press the frame in place to adhere.

5. Using the pencil and ruler, mark a horizontal line for the caption. Write the caption using the white pencil.

6. Use the kneaded rubber eraser to erase all pencil marks.

They Lived Happily Ever After

Create elegant photo corners from shrink-plastic tiles. A simple rubber stamp in a floral motif is used to create the delicate pattern.

Materials

- photo
- one 12" x 12" (30.5 cm x 30.5 cm) sheet pink paper
- one 9" x 12" (23 cm x 30.5 cm) sheet straw paper
- one 9" x 12" (23 cm x 30.5 cm) sheet cream textured paper
- one 9" x 12"(23 cm x 30.5 cm) sheet shrink plastic
- two or three floral rubber stamps
- black inkpad
- double-sided adhesive sheet, such as Peel-N-Stick
- archival-quality adhesive spray
- archival-quality tape
- colored pencils in the following colors: white, cream, and pink (Prisma Colors work best)

Tools

- tracing paper
- metal-edged ruler
- craft knife
- scissors
- pencil
- kneaded rubber eraser
- black fine-tip marker

Instructions

1. Use the tracing paper to make the template for the corner piece. From the shrink plastic, make four corner pieces. With the black ink, stamp the floral designs in a random pattern on the rough side of the corner pieces. Let dry. Leaving some spaces open, color in the remaining spaces with the colored pencils. Following the manufacturer's directions, bake the shrink plastic. Let cool.

2. Using the ruler and knife, trim the straw paper to 7 1/2" x 9 1/2" (19 cm x 24 cm). Cut a 5 1/4" x 7 1/4" (13.5 cm x 18.5 cm) window in the center of the trimmed paper to make a mat. Trim the photo to 6" x 8" (15 cm x 20.5 cm). Tape the photo to the back of the mat using the archival-quality tape. Place the matted photo 3/4" (2 cm) from the top edge, and 1 3/8" (3.5 cm) from the left edge of the pink paper. Use the

pencil to lightly mark the pink paper at the corners of the matted photo for placement. Following the manufacturer's directions, coat the back of the matted photo with adhesive spray. Press in place.

3. Print a title or a personal sentiment on the cream textured paper using the pencil. Center the title, and trim the cream paper to 2 1/2" x 5 1/2" (6.5 cm x 14 cm). Tear the right edge of the title box. Coat the back of the title box with adhesive spray. Referring to the photo for placement, press in place next to the photo.

4. Use the marker to write the names and date.

5. Use the kneaded rubber eraser to remove all pencil marks.

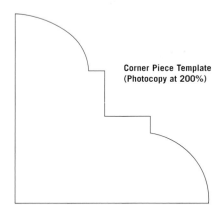

Corner Piece Template (Photocopy at 200%)

6. Using a finished plastic corner as a pattern, cut four corner pieces from the double-sided adhesive sheet. Peel off the protective paper, and attach the adhesive sheet to the shiny side of the corners. Remove the remaining protective paper, and overlapping the mat approximately 1/2" (1 cm), press the corners in place.

Yarn Painting

Remember reading *Pat the Bunny*? Half the fun was in touching the soft accents added to the book's shiny pages. Add tactile elements to your pages with soft yarn. Mexican folk artists use colorful strands of yarn as paint. They embed it into beeswax to illustrate enchanting stories and to record historical events. Now you can paint with twisted, turned, and coiled yarn. Because the yarn is secured with double-sided adhesive rather than with beeswax, small yarn accents work best. Take advantage of the beautiful color selection and the inviting texture of yarn.

Sample 1. Cut a wavy horizontal line from the double-sided adhesive. Remove the protective paper to expose the adhesive, and cover it with similar types of yarn.

Sample 2. Add paper leaves and stems.

Sample 3. Top the stems with blossoms of coiled yarn.

Summer Fun

Warm-colored yarn trim makes this affectionate sun even warmer.
Easy coils make all the difference.

Materials

- photos
- one 12" x 12" (30.5 cm x 30.5 cm) sheet khaki paper
- one 8 1/2" x 11" (21.5 cm x 28 cm) sheet yellow paper
- one 8 1/2" x 11" (21.5 cm x 28 cm) sheet orange paper
- double-sided adhesive sheet, such as Peel-N-Stick
- white craft glue
- archival-quality adhesive spray
- light blue, brown, and pink pencils
- yellow yarn
- purple chisel-tip marker
- black fine-tip marker

Tools

- scissors
- toothpick
- craft knife
- metal-edged ruler
- pencil
- tracing paper
- kneaded rubber eraser

Instructions

1. Using the ruler and knife, trim all photos to 3 1/4" x 4 3/4" (8.5 cm x 12 cm). Place the top photo 1 1/2" (4 cm) from the right edge and 1 3/8" (3.5 cm) from the top edge of the khaki paper. Place the bottom-right photo 1 1/2" (4 cm) from the right edge and 3/4" (2 cm) from the bottom edge of the khaki paper. Aligning the top and the bottom edges, place the bottom-left photo 3/8" (1 cm) from the bottom-right photo. Use the pencil to lightly mark the khaki paper at the corners of the photos for placement. Following the manufacturer's directions, coat the backs of the photos with adhesive spray. Press the photos in place.

2. On the double-sided adhesive sheet, draw 12 circles, each 5/8" (1.5 cm) in diameter. Peel off the protective paper from the circles, and, allowing at least 1/2" (1 cm) between each circle, attach them to the yellow paper. Remove the remaining protective paper from one circle to expose the adhesive. Cut one 8" (20.5 cm) length of yarn. Place one end of the yarn in the center of the circle, and using the toothpick or knife, press to adhere. Working from the center out, coil the yarn to match the adhesive circle, and press to adhere. When complete, trim the end of the yarn. Use the toothpick to apply a small amount of white craft glue to the end of the yarn, and attach it to coiled circle. Hold the end in place until glue is dry. Repeat for remaining the circles. Trim the yellow paper around the circles.

3. Use the tracing paper to make the templates for the sun face. (See Sun template on page 106.) Cut the shapes from the corresponding colors of paper. Coat the back of the scalloped edge with adhesive spray, and press it in place on the sun face. Use the colored pencils to draw the face on the sun. Referring to the photo for shading, shade the eyelids, the nose, and the cheeks. Place the sun face 2 3/4" (7 cm) from the left edge and 1 7/8" (5 cm) from the top edge of the khaki paper. Use the pencil to mark the khaki paper at the top and the bottom of the sun face for placement. Coat the back of the sun face with adhesive spray. Press in place. Coat the backs of the yarn circles with adhesive spray. Place the yarn circles around the sun face, and press to adhere.

4. Write the title using the purple chisel-tip marker. Use the black fine-tip marker to write the captions under the photos.

5. Use the kneaded rubber eraser to remove all pencil marks.

Tropical Retreat

This versatile medium can suggest grass, bark, and even coconuts.

Materials

- photos
- one 12" x 12" (30.5 cm x 30.5 cm) sheet tan paper
- one 8¹/₂" x 11" (21.5 cm x 28 cm) sheet gray paper
- one 8¹/₂" x 11" (21.5 cm x 28 cm) sheet green paper
- one 8¹/₂" x 11" (21.5 cm x 28 cm) sheet green patterned paper
- one 8¹/₂" x 11" (21.5 cm x 28 cm) sheet rust paper
- double-sided adhesive sheet, such as Peel-N-Stick
- white craft glue
- archival-quality adhesive spray
- brown, tan, and pale green yarn
- green broad-tip marker

Tools

- scissors
- toothpick
- craft knife
- metal-edged ruler
- pencil
- tracing paper
- kneaded rubber eraser

Instructions

1. Using the ruler and knife, trim the photos to the following sizes, from the top down: 5" x 3¹/₂" (12.5 cm x 9 cm), 5³/₄" x 3¹/₂" (14.5 cm x 9 cm), and 5³/₄" x 3¹/₂" (14.5 cm x 9 cm). Referring to the photo for placement, arrange the photos on the tan paper. Use the pencil to lightly mark the tan paper at the corners of the photos for placement. Following the manufacturer's directions, coat the backs of the photos with adhesive spray. Press the photos in place.

2. Use the tracing paper to make the palm tree templates. (See Palm Tree template on page 106.) Cut the shapes from the corresponding colors.

3. Referring to the broken lines on the palm tree pattern, draw three trunk stripes on the double-sided adhesive sheet. Peel off the protective paper, and attach the adhesive shapes to the large trunk shape, where indicated. Remove the remaining protective paper from the stripes to expose the adhesive. Cut 1¹/₂" (4 cm) lengths of tan yarn. Center and place the yarn lengths side by side on the adhesive sheet until it is covered. Use the scissors to trim the ends of the yarn flush with the sides of the trunk. Place the large trunk shape

1" (2.5 cm) from the bottom edge and 2³/₄" (7 cm) from the right edge of the tan paper. Referring to the photo, place the remaining pattern pieces on the tan paper. Use the pencil to mark the tan paper at chosen reference points on the tree for placement. Coat the backs of the pattern pieces with adhesive spray. Press the pieces in place.

4. Draw three circles ⁵/₈" (1.5 cm) in diameter on the double-sided adhesive sheet. Peel off the protective paper from the circles, and attach them to the rust paper, allowing at least ¹/₂" (1 cm) between each circle. Remove the remaining protective paper from one circle to expose the adhesive. Cut one 8" (20.5 cm) length of yarn. Place one end of the yarn in the center of the circle, and press with a toothpick or knife to adhere. Working from the center out, coil the yarn around the adhesive circle, then press to adhere. When complete, trim the end of the yarn. Use the toothpick to apply a small amount of white craft glue to the end of the yarn, and attach it to the coiled circle. Hold the end in place until glue is dry. Repeat for the remaining circles. Trim the rust paper around the circles. Coat the backs of the circles with the adhesive

spray. Referring to the photo for placement, press the yarn circles in place.

5. From the double-sided adhesive sheet, cut eight ¹/₁₆" (0.2 cm)-wide strips of varying lengths. Peel off the protective paper from the strips. Referring to the photo, attach the strips to the tan paper. Remove the remaining protective paper from the strips to expose the adhesive. From the pale green yarn, cut eight 2¹/₂" (6.5 cm) lengths. Place the yarn lengths on the adhesive strips, and press to adhere. Use the scissors to cut the ends of the yarn lengths to match the adhesive strips. From the double-sided adhesive sheet, cut two ¹/₁₆" (0.2 cm)-wide curved strips, 2" (5 cm) and 2¹/₂" (6.5 cm) in length. Peel off the protective paper from the strips. Referring to the photo, attach strips to the palm fronds. Remove the remaining protective paper from the strips to expose the adhesive. From pale green yarn, cut two 4" (10 cm) lengths. Place the yarn lengths on the adhesive strips, and press to adhere. Use the scissors to cut ends of yarn lengths to match the adhesive strips.

6. Use the marker to write the title.

7. Use the kneaded rubber eraser to remove all pencil marks.

Cross-Stitch

It is hard to believe that beautiful and complex samplers are made by repeating a simple cross-stitch. This basic building block can also be used to adorn scrapbook pages.

To complete a single cross-stitch, bring the needle from the back to the front at the lower-left corner of a cross (a set of four holes). Then insert the needle in the top-right corner of the cross. Refer to Diagram A. Repeat this process, going from the bottom-right corner to the top-left corner to form an X. Each square on the chart represents one complete stitch. Start with 12" to 15" (30.5 cm to 38 cm) lengths of floss. Longer lengths of floss may twist or knot. Use only the number of strands called for in step one. To secure the ends, hold 1" (2.5 cm) of floss at the back of the paper or fabric, and complete the first few cross-stitches over it, securing it in the stitches. To finish, insert the needle through several completed stitches on the back of the paper or fabric. Draw the floss through the stitches, and trim the end. Carry the floss by weaving it into previously completed stitches on the back of the paper or fabric. Remember that any loose threads on the back will show through to the front of the paper or fabric.

Diagram A

Sample 1. After stitching on the perforated paper, carefully cut around the image to create a delicate appliqué.

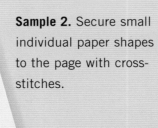

Sample 2. Secure small individual paper shapes to the page with cross-stitches.

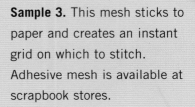

Sample 3. This mesh sticks to paper and creates an instant grid on which to stitch. Adhesive mesh is available at scrapbook stores.

By the Bay

For stitching, perforated paper is a great alternative to even-weave cross-stitch fabric. It is made from heavy paper stock and resists crinkling or tearing. And because it won't unravel like fabric, you don't have to finish the edges.

Materials

- photos
- one 12" x 12" (30.5 cm x 30.5 cm) sheet blue polka-dot paper
- one 8½" x 11" (21.5 cm x 28 cm) sheet burgundy patterned paper
- cable-car ticket or postcard
- ticket stub
- 14-count white perforated paper
- embroidery floss in the following colors: light blue, brown, pink, and white
- brown chisel-tip marker
- archival-quality adhesive spray

Tools

- scissors
- #10 sharp crewel needle
- craft knife
- metal-edged ruler
- line-art alphabet
- pencil
- tracing paper
- embroidery needle
- kneaded rubber eraser

Instructions

1. Using three strands of embroidery floss and referring to Diagram A, cross-stitch the sailboat on the perforated paper. Using the ruler and knife, trim the perforated paper to 2¼" x 4¾" (6 cm x 12 cm).

2. Trim the large photo to 6¾" x 4¼" (17 cm x 11 cm) and the small photo to 4⅛" x 3⅜" (10.5 cm x 8.5 cm). Place the large photo 1" (2.5 cm) from the bottom edge and ¾" (2 cm) from the left edge of the polka-dot paper. Overlapping the top corner of large photo, place the small photo 1½" (4 cm) from the right edge and 3¾" (9.5 cm) from the bottom edge of the polka-dot paper. Referring to the photo for placement, set the ticket, the ticket stub, and the cross-stitch sailboat on the polka-dot paper. Note: Because sizes may vary, adjust as needed, keeping all items at right angles. Use the pencil to lightly mark the polka-dot paper at the corners of the photos, the ticket, the ticket stub, and the cross-stitch sailboat for placement. Following the manufacturer's directions, coat the backs of all items with adhesive. Place them on the polka-dot paper, and press to adhere.

3. From line-art alphabet, enlarge an uppercase letter to 2¾" (7 cm) tall. Make a pattern for the letter on tracing paper. From the burgundy patterned paper, cut out the letter. Place the letter 1¼" (3 cm) from the left edge and 2¾" (7 cm) from the top edge of the polka-dot paper. Use the pencil to mark the polka-dot paper at the corners of the letter for placement. Coat the back of the letter with adhesive spray. Press in place.

4. Use the brown chisel-tip marker to write the title.

5. Use the kneaded rubber eraser to remove all pencil marks.

Diagram A

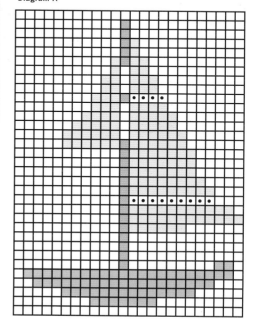

Graduation Day, 1922

Waste canvas is even-weave canvas basted onto non-even-weave fabric to provide a grid for cross-stitching. After stitching, gently remove the waste canvas threads with tweezers.

Materials

- photo
- 12" x 12" (30.5 cm x 30.5 cm) sheet mauve patterned paper
- 8½" x 11" (21.5 cm x 28 cm) sheet light pink paper
- 8½" x 11" (21.5 cm x 28 cm) sheet pink patterned paper
- 8½" x 11" (21.5 cm x 28 cm) sheet green paper
- 6" x 12" (15 cm x 30.5 cm) rectangle pink print fabric
- 28" (71 cm) length ³⁄₈" (1 cm)-wide green satin ribbon
- 14-count waste canvas
- antique postcard
- embroidery floss in light pink, medium pink, dark pink, and green
- spray starch
- archival-quality adhesive spray
- black fine-tip marke

Tools

- tracing paper
- scissors
- #9 embroidery needle
- small embroidery hoop (optional)
- tweezers
- iron
- craft knife
- metal-edged ruler
- kneaded rubber eraser

Instructions

1. Photocopy Diagram A, and make a template using the tracing paper. Center the pattern on the right side of the fabric, and use the pencil to trace lightly around the pattern.

2. From the waste canvas, cut five 4" (10 cm) squares. Referring to the photo for placement, center and baste one square on the top of the fabric strip. Place the fabric in the embroidery hoop, if desired. Using two strands of embroidery floss and stitching through both the fabric and the waste canvas, cross-stitch one flower (refer to Diagram B). Use the tweezers to carefully remove the waste canvas one thread at a time from behind the stitching. Pull out the threads parallel to the fabric. Do not pull at an angle, or you may loosen the cross-stitches. Repeat for the remaining flowers. Rotate the waste canvas squares before basting to change the direction of the flowers. (Three flowers are stitched with only the bottom leaf.)

3. Coat the back with spray starch. Use an iron to press the fabric. Use the scissors to trim the fabric strip along the marked lines. Coat the back of the fabric with adhesive spray. Align the right edge of fabric strip to the short side of the light pink paper, and press to adhere. From the green

paper, make a ³⁄₈" x 5½" (1 cm x 14 cm) strip with one torn side. Coat the back with adhesive spray. Referring to the photo for placement, set the straight side next to the fabric strip. Press to adhere. Using the ruler and knife, trim the overlapping strip. From the pink patterned paper, make one 1½" x 4" x 4" (4 cm x 10 cm x 10 cm) triangle. Coat the back with adhesive spray. Referring to the photo for placement, press the triangle next to the fabric strip.

4. Trim the photo to 4⁵⁄₈" x 3⁵⁄₈" (11.5 cm x 9 cm). Place the photo diagonally, with the lower-left corner 1" (2.5 cm) from the bottom edge and the lower-right corner 1⁷⁄₈" (5 cm) from the bottom edge of the pink paper. Mark the pink paper at the corners for placement. Coat the back with adhesive spray. Press in place. Place the pink paper ¼" (0.6 cm) from the right edge and 3" (7.5 cm) from the top edge of the mauve patterned paper. Mark the mauve paper at the corners for placement. Coat the back with adhesive spray. Press in place. Referring to the photo for placement, set the bottom edge of the postcard parallel to the top edge of the photo. Mark the pink and mauve papers at the corners for placement. Coat the back with adhesive spray. Press in place.

5. Coat the back of the ribbon with adhesive spray. Overlap the photo and keep the ribbon parallel to the fabric border; press in place. Wrap the ribbon around the back of the mauve paper; press in place. Bring the ribbon to the front of the pink paper, press the end of ribbon parallel to the photo. Fold the end of the ribbon in a loop, and press in place on the pink paper. Use the scissors to trim the ends.

6. Use the black marker to write the caption. Use the eraser to remove pencil marks.

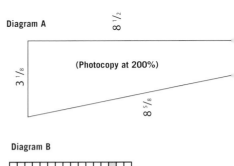

Diagram A

8 ½

3 ⅛   (Photocopy at 200%)

8 ⅝

Diagram B

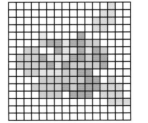

- ☐ Light Pink
- ☐ Medium Pin
- ☐ Dark Pink
- ☐ Green

Quilting

Papercrafters have discovered the age-old art of quilting. Everybody loves quilts, and now you can sew a soft block to smooth paper or stitch up a quilted vignette. If you can use scissors and thread a needle, then you can add a puffy fabric design to a page. Browse through quilt books for inspiration, and choose from hundreds of traditional block designs. By introducing the patterns and textures of fabric, you can make any page layout more interesting and more inviting.

Sample 2. Pin the templates to the selected fabrics, and cut out the shapes.

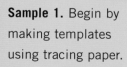

Sample 1. Begin by making templates using tracing paper.

Sample 3. Using a running stitch, stitch the fabric shapes to the paper.

County Fair

Mom, apple pie, county fairs, and quilts.

Materials

- photos
- one 12" x 12" (30.5 cm x 30.5 cm) sheet wheat paper
- archival-quality adhesive spray
- archival-quality tape
- scraps of fabric in the following colors: tan, tan print, gold print, red print, brown print, blue, light blue print, medium blue print, and dark blue print
- red thread
- polyester batting
- blue pencil
- letter stickers

Tools

- craft knife
- metal-edged ruler
- pencil
- tracing paper
- scissors
- needle
- kneaded rubber eraser

Instructions

1. Using the ruler and knife, trim the photos to 4¹/₂" x 3¹/₂" (11.5 cm x 9 cm). Place the top photo 1" (2.5 cm) from the right edge and 1" (2.5 cm) from the top edge of the wheat paper. Overlapping the corner of the top photo, place the bottom photo 2³/₄" (7 cm) from the left edge and 4" (10 cm) from the top edge of the wheat paper. Use the pencil to lightly mark the wheat paper at the corners of the photos for placement. Following the manufacturer's directions, coat the backs of the photos with adhesive spray. Press the photos in place to adhere.

2. From the red fabric, cut one 5¹/₄" x ⁷/₈" (13.5 cm x 2 cm) strip. Use the tracing paper to make the template for the zigzag border. (See Zigzag Border template on page 104.) From the tan print fabric, cut one zigzag shape. Place the red strip 1" (2.5 cm) from the right edge and 1" (2.5 cm) from the top edge of the wheat paper. Place the zigzag strip over the red strip. Stitch over and under (running stitch) through the paper and the fabric along the top of the strip. Secure the ends of the thread to the back of the paper using the archival-quality tape. Trim the ends. Repeat along the center of the zigzag shape.

3. Make the templates for Block A. (See Block A template on page 107.) Cut the shapes from the corresponding fabrics. Using a running stitch, stitch the small squares to the large square. From the batting, cut one 3¹/₄" (8.5 cm) square. Aligning the right side of batting with the right side of the top photo, place the batting below the photo. Center and place Block A on the batting. Stitch through all of the layers around the outside edge of the block. Secure the ends of the thread to the back of the paper with the archival-quality tape. Trim the ends.

4. Make the templates for Block B. (See Block B template on page 107.) Cut the shapes from the corresponding fabrics. Note: A ¹/₄" (0.6 cm) seam allowance should be added to the center pieces because they overlap each other slightly. Stitch the small strips to the center square. Stitch the large strips to the small strips. Place Block B 2¹/₄" (6 cm) from the right edge and 1¹/₂" (4 cm) from the bottom edge of the wheat paper. Stitch through all of the layers around the outside edge of the block. Secure the ends of the thread to the back of the paper with archival-quality tape. Trim the ends.

5. Attach the stickers. Write the captions using the blue pencil.

6. Use the kneaded rubber eraser to remove all pencil marks.

Sweet Dreams

When introducing large areas of color, try sewing on a scrap of fabric instead of paper. Also try securing design elements with a few well-placed quilting stitches instead of adhesives.

Materials

- photo
- one 12" x 12" (30.5 cm x 30.5 cm) sheet blue paper
- 8 1/2" x 11" (21.5 cm x 28 cm) sheet cream paper
- archival-quality adhesive spray
- archival-quality tape
- scrap of yellow fabric
- 9" (23 cm) dark blue fabric
- white thread
- polyester fiber fill
- white craft glue
- blue broad-tip marker
- black fine-tip marker

Tools

- pencil
- tracing paper
- scissors
- metal-edged ruler
- needle
- craft knife
- toothpick
- kneaded rubber eraser

Instructions

1. Using the tracing paper, make the templates for the star and the moon. (See Moon and Star templates on page 108.) Cut the shapes from the corresponding fabrics. Place the sky 3/4" (2 cm) from the right edge and 1/4" (0.6 cm) from the top edge of the blue paper. Separate the fiberfill into two small clumps. Referring to the photo for placement, set one clump in the center of the sky and one clump in the corner of the sky. Place the moon shape over the center clump of the fiberfill. Stitch over and under (running stitch) through all layers around the moon shape. Secure the ends of the thread to the back of the paper using the archival-quality tape. Trim the ends. Above the moon shape, stitch free-form, horizontal lines in the sky, securing the second clump of fiberfill in the stitching. Below the moon shape, stitch a free-form, horizontal line in the sky. Secure the ends of the thread to the back of the paper using the archival-quality tape. Trim the ends. Use the toothpick to apply a small amount of craft glue to the wrong side of the fabric at the edges of the sky. Hold in place until the glue dries.

2. Trim the cream paper to 5 3/4" x 4 3/4" (14.5 cm x 12 cm). Center and cut a 4 1/4" x 3 1/4" (11 cm x 8.5 cm) window in the cream rectangle to make a mat. Using the ruler and the knife, trim the photo to 4 3/4" x 3 3/4" (12 cm x 9.5 cm). Tape the photo to the back of the mat. Place the matted photo 1" (2.5 cm) from the right edge and 1" (2.5 cm) from the bottom edge of the blue paper. Use the pencil to lightly mark the blue paper at the corners of the matted photo for placement. Coat the back of the matted photo with adhesive spray. Press in place.

3. From the cream paper cut one star. Coat the back of the star with adhesive spray. Referring to the photo for placement, press the star in place above the top-right corner of the mat.

4. Write the title using the blue marker. Use the black marker to write the caption.

5. Use the kneaded rubber eraser to remove all pencil marks.

17

Machine-Stitching

This technique is part decoration and all fun. You can use machine-stitching to join layers of paper or to attach embellishments, but the real excitement is with the design possibilities. Use lines of stitching to outline and to contour. So dust off your sewing machine, and use it to enhance your paper art.

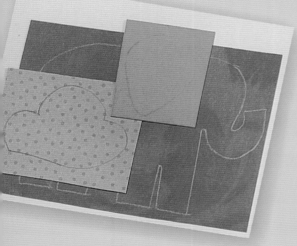

Sample 1. To machine-stitch a small paper design to the page, begin by tracing the shapes onto the selected papers.

Sample 2. Cut out the shapes.

Sample 3. Machine-stitch the large shape to the background paper. Attach the small pieces with double-sided adhesive or with adhesive spray.

Birthday Cake

This page illustration is paper-piecing with a twist. The paper shapes are enhanced by machine-stitching. Review your favorite paper-pieced designs, and enhance them with this decorative application.

Materials

- photos
- one 12" x 12" (30.5 cm x 30.5 cm) sheet tan paper
- one 8½" x 11" (21.5 cm x 28 cm) sheet dark pink paper
- one 8½" x 11" (21.5 cm x 28 cm) sheet light pink paper
- one 8½" x 11" (21.5 cm x 28 cm) sheet purple paper
- one 8½" x 11" (21.5 cm x 28 cm) sheet white-and-yellow striped paper
- one 8½" x 11" (21.5 cm x 28 cm) sheet yellow paper
- one 8½" x 11" (21.5 cm x 28 cm) sheet blue patterned paper
- magenta cellophane streamer
- white thread
- purple pencil
- black fine-tip marker
- archival-quality adhesive spray
- archival-quality tape
- double-sided adhesive sheet, such as Peel-N-Stick

Tools

- scissors
- sewing machine
- metal-edged ruler
- craft knife
- pencil
- tracing paper
- kneaded rubber eraser

Instructions

1. Use the tracing paper to make the templates for the cake, plate, and candles. (See Cake, Plate, and Candles template on page 108.) Although areas of the scalloping are covered by layering, make it one piece. Cut the shapes from the corresponding colors. Referring to the photo for placement, arrange the plate and the base of the cake on the tan paper. Machine-stitch around the sides and the bottom of the base of the cake. Place the scalloping on the base of the cake, and place the top of the cake on the scallop. Machine-stitch around the top of the cake. Carefully pull the ends of the thread to the back of the paper, and secure them with archival-quality tape. Trim the ends. Place the candles and the flames on the cake. Use the pencil to mark lightly the tan paper at the tops of the flames for placement. From the double-sided adhesive sheet, cut ⅛" (0.3 cm)-wide strips. Trim the strips to fit the backs of the candles and the flames. Peel off the protective paper, and attach the adhesive to the backs of the candles and the flames. Remove the remaining protective paper, and press the candles and the flames in place to adhere.

2. Referring to the photo for placement, arrange the streamer on the top-left corner of the tan paper. Machine-stitch over the streamer to secure it. Pull the ends of the thread to the back of the paper, and secure them with tape. Trim the ends.

3. Using the ruler and knife, trim the right photo to 3⅛" x 4⅝" (8 cm x 11.5 cm). Place the photo 1½" (4 cm) from the right edge and 2¾" (7 cm) from the bottom edge of the tan paper. Use the pencil to mark the tan paper at the corners of the photo for placement. Following the manufacturer's directions, coat the back of the photo with adhesive spray. Press in place. Trim the left photo to 5¼" x 3½" (13.5 cm x 9 cm). Overlapping the right photo, place the photo 2¼" (6 cm) from the left edge and 1½" (4 cm) from the bottom edge of the tan paper. Use the pencil to mark the tan paper at the corners of the photo for placement. Coat the back of the photo with adhesive spray. Press in place.

4. Use the purple pencil to write Happy Birthday on the cake plate. Use the marker to write the caption.

5. Use the kneaded rubber eraser to remove all pencil marks.

Paper Horizon

All of the paper edges in this arrangement, with the exception of the trimmed edge of the mat, are torn. Tearing the shapes makes them soft and irregular. Machine-stitching enhances the meandering nature of the paper shapes.

Materials

- photo
- one 12" x 12" (30.5 cm x 30.5 cm) sheet ivory paper
- one 12" x 12" (30.5 cm x 30.5 cm) sheet blue print vellum
- one 8 1/2" x 11" (21.5 cm x 28 cm) sheet blue patterned paper
- one 8 1/2" x 11" (21.5 cm x 28 cm) sheet silver paper
- one 8 1/2" x 11" (21.5 cm x 28 cm) sheet cream paper
- one 8 1/2" x 11" (21.5 cm x 28 cm) sheet white paper
- one brown paper sack
- white tissue paper
- 12" x 6" (30.5 cm x 15 cm) piece purple sheer fabric
- white thread
- navy blue thread
- archival-quality adhesive spray
- archival-quality tape

Tools

- scissors
- sewing machine
- metal-edged ruler
- craft knife
- pencil

Instructions

1. With the pencil, print the title on the blue patterned paper.

2. From the tissue paper, the silver paper, and the cream paper, tear several hill shapes. From the paper sack, tear a road shape. From the blue print fabric, tear two small cloud shapes. Tear a large cloud shape around the title printed on the blue patterned paper.

3. Place the fabric on the top half of the vellum. Referring to the photo for placement, arrange the torn shapes on the vellum. Using the white thread and straight and zigzag stitches, machine-stitch over the shapes to secure them to the vellum. Using the navy thread and a zigzag stitch, stitch a broken line in the center of the road.

4. Using the ruler and knife, trim the photo to 3 3/4" x 5 1/4" (9.5 cm x 13.5 cm). Trim the white paper to 4 1/2" x 6" (11.5 cm x 15 cm). Center and cut a 3 1/4" x 4 3/4" (8.5 cm x 12 cm) window in the white rectangle to make a mat. Tape the photo to the back of the mat. Place the matted photo 1" (2.5 cm) from the right edge and 3/4" (2 cm) from the bottom edge of the vellum paper. Using the white thread and a straight and a zigzag stitch, stitch the mat to the vellum. Carefully pull the ends of the thread to the back of the paper, and secure them with archival-quality tape. Trim the ends.

5. Following the manufacturer's directions, coat the back of the vellum. Place the vellum on the ivory paper, and press to adhere.

Found-Object Collage

Bits of lace, luggage tags, feathers, old jewelry, paper labels, shoelaces, matchbooks, and chop sticks. Why include this curious list in a scrapbook recipe? One of these things may be the perfect accent to add to your scrapbook page. The fun of found-object art is incorporating something quirky or unexpected into a composition of otherwise flat component parts. So before your next scrapping session begins, hunt through your sewing box or your junk drawer. You will be surprised at what you will find.

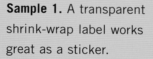

Sample 1. A transparent shrink-wrap label works great as a sticker.

Sample 2. Pin a romantic message to a special page using a gold safety pin.

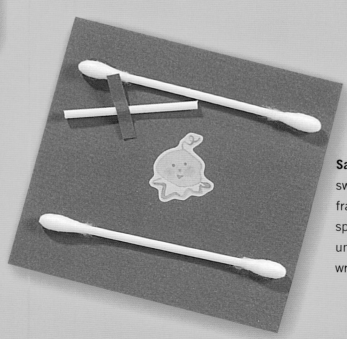

Sample 3. Fashion cotton swabs into a unique frame for baby. Use a spot of white craft glue under each cotton-wrapped end.

Nature's Canopy

Gather a handful of colorful leaves, and press them between the pages of a heavy book. Dried leaves look great bordering artwork or outdoor photos.

Materials

- artwork
- 12" x 12" (30.5 cm x 30.5 cm) sheet green patterned paper
- scraps of rust paper
- award ribbon
- dried leaves
- twigs
- white milky pen
- archival-quality adhesive spray
- double-sided adhesive sheet

Tools

- craft knife
- metal-edged ruler
- pencil
- kneaded rubber eraser

Instructions

1. Using the ruler and knife, trim the artwork to 8 1/2" x 10 1/2" (21.5 cm x 26.5 cm). Place the artwork diagonally with the top left corner 1" (2.5 cm) and the top right corner 1/4" (0.6 cm) from the top edge of the green paper. Use the pencil to mark lightly the green paper at the corners of the artwork for placement. Following the manufacturer's directions, coat the back of the art work with adhesive spray. Place the artwork on the green paper, and press to adhere.

2. From the double-sided adhesive sheet, cut 1" x 2" (2.5 cm x 5 cm) rectangle. Peel off the protective paper, and attach the adhesive lengthwise to the back of the ribbon, directly below the eyelet. Remove the remaining protective paper; referring to the photo for placement, press the ribbon in place.

3. Coat the backs of the dried leaves with adhesive spray. Arrange them on and around the artwork as desired. From the double-sided adhesive sheet, cut one

3/16" x 7" (0.5 cm x 18 cm) strip. Peel the protective paper, and attach the strip to the back of the rust paper. Trim the paper to match the adhesive. Cut the strip into seven lengths. Peel the remaining protective paper from the adhesive strips. Place the strips over the twigs at selected points to secure the twigs to the artwork.

4. Write the caption using the white milky pen.

5. Use the kneaded rubber eraser to remove all pencil marks.

Little Boy Collage

Empty the contents of your 9-year-old's pockets, and you will have the makings for a great page layout. This is a case in which art definitely imitates life.

Materials

- photo
- one 12" x 12" (30.5 cm x 30.5 cm) sheet oatmeal paper
- one 8 1/2" x 11 (21.5 cm x 28 cm) sheet blue patterned paper
- assorted flat objects
- archival-quality adhesive spray
- double-sided adhesive sheet, such as Peel-N-Stick

Tools

- craft knife
- metal-edged ruler
- pencil
- kneaded rubber eraser
- black fine-tip marker (optional)

Instructions

1. On the blue patterned paper, use the marker to print the title (or do this on a computer). Using the ruler and the knife, center the title and trim the blue patterned paper to 3" x 10" (7.5 cm x 25.5 cm). Place the title box 1/8" (0.3 cm) from the right edge and 3/8" (1 cm) from the top edge of the oatmeal paper. Use the pencil to lightly mark the oatmeal paper at the corners of the title box for placement. Following the manufacturer's directions, coat the back of the title box with adhesive spray. Press in place.

2. Trim the photo to 5" x 6 1/2" (12.5 cm x 16.5 cm). Place it diagonally with the top-left corner 1 3/4" (4.5 cm) and the top right corner 3/4" (2 cm) from the top edge of the oatmeal paper. Use the pencil to mark the oatmeal paper at the corners of the photo for placement. Coat the back of the photo with adhesive spray. Press in place.

3. Referring to the photo, arrange selected items on the page as desired. Mark the oatmeal paper at desired points on the items for placement. Attach the items to oatmeal paper. Paper items can be attached with adhesive spray, and plastic or fiber items can be attached with the double-sided adhesive sheet.

4. Use the kneaded rubber eraser to remove all pencil marks.

Paper-Piecing

Paper-piecing consists of cutting shapes from colored paper and arranging the individual shapes to make a complete design. It is usually done in one of two ways. One version requires that some pieces in the composition overlap each other. It is necessary to allow for excess paper along the edges that will be covered by another layer of paper. When layering, remember to overlap when making the templates. With the second version, the pieces fit together like the pieces of a puzzle, with no overlap. These pieces are usually simple geometric shapes, such as squares and rectangles. Because the pieces fit together snugly, care should be taken to cut the pieces as accurately as possible.

The finished compositions are made of flat areas of color, so paper-piecing resembles silk screening done by fine artists or appliqué done by quilters. In fact, many paper-piecing patterns are borrowed from line art intended for iron-on or needle-turned appliqué.

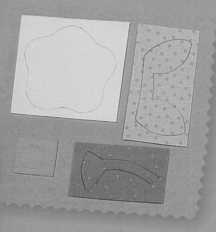

Sample 1. Make the patterns for the design, and trace the shapes onto the selected papers.

Sample 2. Cut out the shapes.

Sample 3. Layer the shapes, and attach them to the page with adhesive.

Housewarming House

This warm and welcoming house tag is made from simple geometric shapes. The finished tag could be used as a greeting card or as a gift tag.

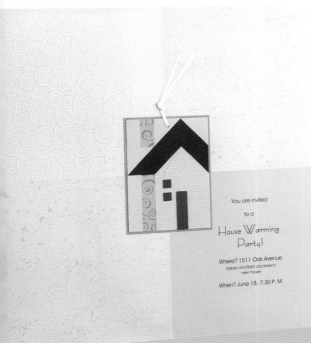

Materials

- one 12" x 12" (30.5 cm x 30.5 cm) sheet white paper
- house-warming announcement
- one 8 1/2" x 11" (21.5 cm x 28 cm) sheet light green patterned paper
- one 8 1/2" x 11" (21.5 cm x 28 cm) sheet mint green patterned paper
- one 8 1/2" x 11" (21.5 cm x 28 cm) sheet gray paper
- one 8 1/2" x 11" (21.5 cm x 28 cm) sheet blue paper
- one 8 1/2" x 11" (21.5 cm x 28 cm) sheet pink paper
- one 8 1/2" x 11" (21.5 cm x 28 cm) sheet pink patterned paper
- one 8 1/2" x 11" (21.5 cm x 28 cm) sheet brown paper
- one 8 1/2" x 11" (21.5 cm x 28 cm) sheet black paper
- one 8 1/2" x 11" (21.5 cm x 28 cm) sheet pink pearlescent paper
- archival-quality adhesive spray
- white craft glue

Tools

- tracing paper
- scissors
- craft knife
- metal-edged ruler
- pencil
- toothpick
- kneaded rubber eraser

Instructions

1. Use the tracing paper to make the templates for the house. (See House template on page 107.) Note: The windows and the door are the only overlapping pieces. The remaining pieces fit together with the sides flat against each other. Therefore, cut these pieces as accurately as possible. Cut the shapes from the corresponding papers. Following the manufacturer's directions, coat the backs of the pieces with adhesive spray. Referring to the template, press all the pieces in place on the gray paper. Center the house design. Using the ruler and knife, trim the gray paper to 3 1/4" x 4 1/4" (8.5 cm x 11 cm). Center the

hole punch 3/8" (1 cm) from the top edge of the gray paper, and punch a hole in the sky. From the pink pearlescent paper, cut one 1/4" x 9" (0.6 cm x 23 cm) strip. Thread the strip through the hole, and carefully knot the ends together. Trim the ends, if necessary.

2. Trim the announcement to 6" x 6" (15 cm x 15 cm). From the light green patterned paper, make one 6" (15 cm) square. From the mint green paper, make two 6" (15 cm) squares. Coat the backs of the squares with adhesive spray. Referring to the photo for placement, press the squares into place on the white paper.

3. Coat the back of the house tag with adhesive spray. Center it on the intersecting corners, and press in place to adhere. Press the knotted strip flat. Use the toothpick to apply a small amount of white craft glue to the back of the strip, and press in place.

Lily of the Valley

This pair of flower sprigs serves as the perfect symmetrical embellishment for an oval mat.

Materials

- photo
- one 12" x 12" (30.5 cm x 30.5 cm) sheet light blue paper
- one 8 1/2" x 11" (21.5 cm x 28 cm) khaki mat with 4 1/2" x 6 1/2" (11 cm x 17 cm) oval window
- one 8 1/2" x 11" (21.5 cm x 28 cm) sheet pink paper
- one 8 1/2" x 11" (21.5 cm x 28 cm) sheet cream paper
- one 8 1/2" x 11" (21.5 cm x 28 cm) sheet mint paper
- one 8 1/2" x 11" (21.5 cm x 28 cm) sheet olive patterned paper
- four 1/8" (0.3 cm)-wide pink sticker borders
- purple pencil
- black fine-tip marker
- archival-quality tape
- archival-quality adhesive spray

Tools

- pencil
- tracing paper
- scissors
- craft knife
- metal-edged ruler
- kneaded rubber eraser

Instructions

1. Using the ruler and knife, trim the photo to 5 1/2" x 7 1/2" (14 cm x 19 cm). Center the oval, and trim the mat to 7 3/4" x 9 5/8" (20 cm x 24.5 cm). Tape the photo to the back of the mat. Place the matted photo 2 1/8" (5.5 cm) from the right edge and 1" (2.5 cm) from the top edge of the light blue paper. Use the pencil to lightly mark the light blue paper at the corners of the mat for placement. Following the manufacturer's directions, coat the back of the matted photo with adhesive spray. Press in place.

2. Use the tracing paper to make the templates for the flowers and the leaves. (See Flowers and Leaves template on page 106.) Cut the shapes from the corresponding colors. Reverse the templates, and cut a second set of shapes in the mirror image of the first set. Referring to the photo for placement, arrange leaves and flowers on the bottom corners of the mat. Use the pencil to lightly mark the light blue paper at the chosen reference points on the flowers and the stems for placement. Coat the backs of the flowers and the leaves with adhesive spray. Press in place.

3. Use the colored pencil to draw the details on the mat, the flower centers, and the leaves. Attach the sticker border 1 1/4" (3 cm) from the outside edge of all four sides of the blue paper. Trim the border from the paper-piecing designs. Write the caption using the marker.

4. Use the kneaded rubber eraser to remove all pencil marks.

Stenciling

An art form that is centuries old, stenciling has a novelty and a versatility all its own. The concept is an easy one: create a negative space, or stencil, and fill the space with color. Plastic stencils can be used again and again. Just clean them occasionally, and store them flat. A good stencil can become as indispensable to paper decoration as a good stamp. Stenciling requires no extraordinary skill and is a great way to decorate any flat surface, including scrapbook pages. The projects included in this chapter require hand-cut stencils, but many precut stencils are available at craft and paper stores. Using a precut stencil eliminates the steps of transferring the design to the stencil blank and cutting the stencil.

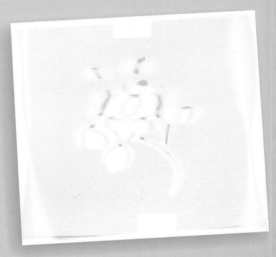

Sample 1. To create a stenciled flower, cut the design from the Ostencil blank. Place the stencil on the paper.

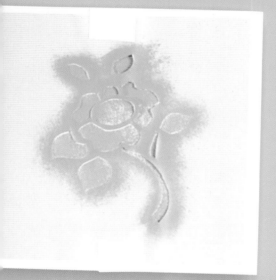

Sample 2. Use the stencil brush to apply a thin coat of paint.

Sample 3. Remove the stencil to reveal the finished flower.

How Do I Love Thee?

A classic floral field serves as the perfect backdrop for a candid wedding photo. Although the difference in value between the paint and the paper is subtle, the pattern is still visible through the tulle sashing.

Materials

- photo
- one 12" x 12" (30.5 cm x 30.5 cm) sheet cream paper
- one 8$^{1}/_{2}$" x 11" (21.5 cm x 28 cm) sheet cream vellum
- one 8$^{1}/_{2}$" x 11" (21.5 cm x 28 cm) sheet white paper
- one 18" x 7" (45.5 cm x 18 cm) strip white tulle
- one stencil blank, 6" x 6" (15 cm x 15 cm) or larger
- white acrylic craft paint
- black fine-tip marker
- archival-quality adhesive spray
- archival-quality tape

Tools

- craft knife
- metal-edged ruler
- pencil
- kneaded rubber eraser
- stencil brush
- paper towel
- scissors
- black fine-tip marker (optional)

Instructions

1. Use the marker to trace the floral stencil design on the stencil blank. (See Floral Motif template on page 107.) Place the stencil blank on a cutting surface, and use a craft knife to cut out each section. Position the stencil on the cream paper. Apply a small amount of the white paint to the tip of the stencil brush. Blot the tip of the brush on the paper towel. Hold the stencil firmly in place with one hand and the brush perpendicular to the paper surface with the other. Lightly touch the paper with the brush, applying the paint with short, pouncing strokes. Repeat this process until the exposed areas are covered with a thin coat of paint. Remove the stencil, and allow the paint to dry. Rotate the paper, stenciling the design in a random pattern until the paper is covered.

2. Using the ruler and knife, trim the photo to 7" x 4$^{3}/_{4}$" (18 cm x 12 cm). Center and place the photo at an angle on the cream paper, with the left corner 2$^{3}/_{4}$" (7 cm) and the right corner 1$^{3}/_{4}$" (4.5 cm) from the top edge of the paper. Use the pencil to lightly mark the cream paper at the corners of the photo for placement. Following the manufacturer's directions, coat the back of the photo with adhesive spray. Press in place.

3. Use the marker or a computer to print a poem or a personal sentiment on the white paper. Center the poem, and trim the white paper to 1$^{1}/_{8}$" x 3$^{1}/_{8}$" (3 cm x 8 cm). Coat the back of the poem box with adhesive spray. Place the poem box below the bottom-left edge of the photo, and press to adhere.

4. From the cream vellum, cut three $^{3}/_{8}$" x 4$^{1}/_{4}$" (1 cm x 11 cm) strips. Referring to the photo for placement, mark three pairs of parallel lines for slits on the cream paper. The slits are $^{1}/_{2}$" (1 cm) long and 1$^{1}/_{4}$" (3 cm) apart. Cut the slits with the craft knife.

5. Lightly coat the tulle with adhesive spray. (Spray only enough to make the fabric slightly tacky so that it will stick to itself when shaped. The spray does not adhere the fabric to the cream paper.) Place the tulle lengthwise on the work surface, and gather in the center and 6" (15 cm) from center on both sides. Manipulate the tulle to the desired shape, and place it on the cream paper. From back to front, thread the vellum strips through the slits and over the top of the gathered sections of tulle to secure it.

6. Working on the backside of the cream paper, pull the strips slightly, and secure the ends of the strips to the back of the paper using the archival-quality tape.

7. Use the scissors to trim the ends of the tulle so that they are flush with the sides of the cream paper.

8. Use the kneaded rubber eraser to remove all pencil marks.

The Great Outdoors

Pay homage to nature and all things wild by adding this row of charming squirrels to your page. A thin coat of stencil paint allows for the faint shading of the tails.

Materials

- photos
- one 12" x 12" (30.5 cm x 30.5 cm) sheet olive patterned paper
- one 12" x 12" (30.5 cm x 30.5 cm) sheet sage patterned paper
- one stencil blank, 6" x 6" (15 cm x 15 cm) or larger
- black fine-tip marker
- brown pencil
- light brown acrylic paint
- medium brown acrylic paint
- archival-quality adhesive spray

Tools

- craft knife
- metal-edged ruler
- pencil
- kneaded rubber eraser
- stencil brush
- paper towel

Instructions

1. Use the marker to trace the squirrel stencil design on the stencil blank. (See Squirrel template on page 109.) Place the stencil blank on the cutting surface, and use a craft knife to cut out each section. Use the pencil to draw a light baseline ⅝" (1.5 cm) from the bottom edge of the sage paper. Position the squirrel body section on the baseline 5" (12.5 cm) from the left edge of the sage paper. Apply a small amount of medium brown paint to the tip of the stencil brush. Blot the tip of the brush on the paper towel. Hold the stencil firmly in place with one hand and the brush perpendicular to the paper surface with the other. Lightly touch the paper with the brush, applying the paint with short, pouncing strokes. Cover the exposed area with a thin coat of paint. Remove the stencil, and allow the paint to dry. Working from right to left, repeat this process with a second and a third body section, allowing 1¼" (3 cm) between each. Align the arms and back-leg section on one of the body sections. Using the medium brown paint, stencil and repeat for remaining bodies. Align the tail section on one of the body sections. Use the light brown acrylic paint to stencil the tail. Repeat to complete three squirrels.

2. Using the ruler and knife, trim the stenciled strip to 11¼" x 3¾" (28.5 cm x 9.5 cm). Tear the top edge of the stenciled strip. Place the strip on the olive paper ¼" (0.6 cm) from the bottom edge, and flush with the right edge of the paper. Use the pencil to lightly mark the olive paper at the corners of the stenciled strip for placement. Following the manufacturer's directions, coat the back of the strip with adhesive spray. Press in place.

3. Trim the photos to the following sizes, from left and moving clockwise: 3¾" x 5½" (9.5 cm x 14 cm), 4¾" x 4" (12 cm x 10 cm), and 4" x 3" (10 cm x 7.5 cm). Referring to the photo for placement, arrange the photos on the olive paper. Use the pencil to lightly mark the olive paper at the corners of the photos for placement. Coat the back of the photos with adhesive spray. Press the photos in place to adhere.

4. Write the text using the brown pencil.

5. Use the kneaded rubber eraser to remove all pencil marks.

recipe # 21

Wrapped Thread

Most scrapbook stores offer yarn, ribbon, twine, and other decorative fibers for use as embellishments. As an interesting alternative to stitching, these threads can be wrapped around frames and simple paper shapes. The enhancement is unique. When selecting materials, keep in mind that the finer the strand, the more subtle the effect. Other non-fiber materials, such as quilling paper, curling ribbon, and twine, can be used for wrapping.

Sample 1. Try wrapping a simple shape with narrow quilling paper strips. Draw a hollow shape on the paper.

Sample 2. Cut out the shape.

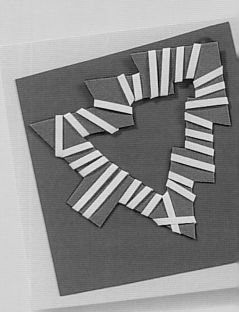

Sample 3. Wrap the shape with the paper strips, and attach the wrapped shape to the background paper.

Once-Upon-a-Time Babies

Pastel floss and metallic pearl cotton highlight the pitted texture of handmade paper.

Materials

- photos
- one 12" x 12" (30.5 cm x 30.5 cm) sheet lavender paper
- one 8½" x 11" (21.5 cm x 28 cm) sheet pale yellow paper
- one small sheet lavender handmade paper
- one small sheet green handmade paper
- one precut blue patterned paper mat, 5⅓" x 6⅝" (13.5 cm x 17 cm) with a 3¼" x 4⅜" (8.5 cm x 11 cm) window
- one purple paper bow
- floral stamp with 1" x 1½" (2.5 cm x 4 cm) image size
- embroidery floss in yellow, green, and lavender
- cream pearl cotton; size 5
- metallic pearl cotton; size 5
- green ink
- brown pencil
- archival-quality adhesive spray
- archival-quality tape

Tools

- craft knife
- metal-edged ruler
- pencil
- scissors
- kneaded rubber eraser

Instructions

1. Using the ruler and knife, trim the yellow paper to 2⅞" x 3¾" (7.5 cm x 9.5 cm). Center and cut a 1⅞" x 2¾" (5 cm x 7 cm) window in the trimmed paper to make a mat. Referring to the photo for placement, set the mat diagonally on the lavender paper with the top-left corner 1⅛" (3 cm) and the top-right corner 1¾" (4.5 cm) from the top edge of the page. Trim the yellow paper to a 3" (7.5 cm) square. Center and cut a 2" (5 cm) square window in the trimmed paper to make a mat. Referring to the photo for placement, set the mat diagonally on the lavender paper with the bottom-left corner ¾" (2 cm) and the bottom-right corner 1¼" (3 cm) from the bottom edge of the page. Mark the lavender paper at the corners of the mats for placement. Following the manufacturer's directions, coat the backs of the mats with the adhesive spray. Place the mats on the lavender paper, and press to adhere.

2. Use the knife to cut a circle 2⅝" (6.5 cm) in diameter from the lavender handmade paper. Center and cut a round window 1¾" (4.5 cm) in diameter in the trimmed paper to make a mat. Cut a 26" (66 cm) length from both the lavender and green flosses. Secure the ends of both lengths to the back of the round mat using the archival-quality tape. Carefully wrap the floss around the mat. Secure the loose ends of the floss to the back of the mat with the

tape. Trim the ends of the floss. Referring to the photo for placement and overlapping the bottom-left corner, place the mat on the large yellow mat. Use the pencil to mark the lavender paper at the top and bottom of the mat for placement. Coat the back of the mat with adhesive spray. Place the mat on the lavender paper and the yellow mat, and press to adhere.

3. Trim the green handmade paper to a 3¼" (8.5 cm) square. Center and cut a 2½" (6.5 cm) square window in trimmed paper to make a mat. From the cream pearl cotton, cut one 20" (51 cm) length. Secure the end of the pearl cotton to the back of the mat with the tape, and carefully wrap it around the mat at selected areas. Secure the loose ends of the pearl cotton to the back of the mat with the tape. Trim the end. Overlapping the small yellow mat, place the green mat 3" (7.5 cm) from the right edge and ¾" (2 cm) from the bottom edge of the lavender paper. Use the pencil to mark the lavender paper at the corners of the mat for placement. Coat the back of the mat with adhesive spray. Place the mat on the lavender paper and press to adhere.

4. Trim the lavender handmade paper to 3⅝" x 2⅞" (9 cm x 7.5 cm). Center and cut a 2⅝" x 1⅞" (6.5 cm x 5 cm) window in the trimmed paper to make a mat. From the metallic pearl cotton, cut two 24" (61 cm) lengths. Secure the end of one length of the pearl cotton to the back

of the mat using tape, and carefully wrap the pearl cotton around the mat at selected areas. Secure the loose ends of the pearl cotton to the back of the mat with tape. Trim the end. Repeat with the second length. Place the lavender mat 1" (2.5 cm) from the left edge and 1¼" (3 cm) from the bottom edge of the lavender paper. Use the pencil to mark the lavender paper at the corners of the mat for placement. Coat the back of the mat with the adhesive spray. Place the mat on the lavender paper, and press to adhere.

5. Place the precut mat 1⅝" (4 cm) from the left edge and ½" (1 cm) from the top edge of the lavender paper. Use the pencil to mark the lavender paper at the corners of the mat for placement. Coat the back of the mat with adhesive spray. Place the mat on the lavender paper, and press to adhere. Coat the back of the paper ribbon with adhesive spray. Press in place above the green mat.

6. Trim the photos so that they are smaller than the mat windows. Coat the backs of the photos with adhesive spray, and press in place inside the mats. With the stamp and the ink, stamp a flower in the round mat. Let dry.

7. Write captions with the brown pencil.

8. Use the kneaded rubber eraser to remove all pencil marks.

A Boy and His Dog

Contrasting fibers make a statement when wrapped around a large and colorful silhouette.

Materials

- photos
- one 12" x 12" (30.5 cm x 30.5 cm) sheet dark green paper
- one 8 1/2" x 11" (21.5 cm x 28 cm) sheet green patterned paper
- one 8 1/2" x 11" (21.5 cm x 28 cm) sheet red paper
- cream yarn
- cream pencil
- archival-quality adhesive spray
- archival-quality tape

Tools

- craft knife
- tracing paper
- metal-edged ruler
- pencil
- scissors
- kneaded rubber eraser
- black fine-tip marker (optional)

Instructions

1. Using the ruler and knife, trim the left photo to 4" x 4" (10 cm x 10 cm). Place it 1 1/2" (4 cm) from the left edge and 3 1/2" (9 cm) from the top edge of the green paper. Trim the right photo to 4" x 6" (10 cm x 15 cm). Place it 2 1/4" (6 cm) from the right edge and 1/4" (0.6 cm) from the top edge of the green paper. Use the pencil to mark the green paper at the corners of the photos for placement. Following the manufacturer's directions, coat the backs of the photos with adhesive spray. Place them on the green paper, and press to adhere.

2. Print the title on the green patterned paper with the marker or on a computer. Tear left, bottom, and right edges of title box to measure 4" x 3" (10 cm x 7.5 cm). Align the title box with the top edge and 1" (2.5 cm) from the left edge of the green paper. Use the pencil to mark the green paper at the corners of the title box for placement. Coat the back of the title box with adhesive spray, and press in place.

3. Use the tracing paper to make the template for the candy cane. (See Candy Cane template on page 103.) From the red paper make five candy canes. From the yarn, cut one 18" (45.5 cm) length. Secure the end of one yarn length to the back of one candy cane using the tape. Wrap it diagonally around the candy cane. Secure the remaining end of the yarn to the back of the candy cane with tape. Trim the end. Wrap the remaining candy canes. Referring to the photo for placement, set the candy canes on the green paper. Use the pencil to mark the green paper at the top and the bottom of each candy cane for placement. Coat the backs of the candy canes with adhesive spray. Press in place.

4. Write the captions with the cream pencil.

5. Use the kneaded rubber eraser to remove all pencil marks.

Gold Leafing

Animal, vegetable, or mineral? Definitely mineral! Gilded urns, picture frames, and statuary look as if they have been dipped in liquid gold. Actually, they have been covered with thinner-than-paper composition gold leaf. Use the same user-friendly material to add a splash of sophistication to a paper scrap. Available at craft or art supply stores, it serves as a quick and stunning accent. Because gold is inherently showy, cover only small areas. Remember that with this technique, less is more.

Sample 2. Create a royal background for small, stamped icons.

Sample 1. Remember the story about the goose that laid the golden egg? Illustrate a fairy tale with these impressive eggs.

Sample 3. Make a paper crown fit for a king.

Moving On

This paper doily once served as a coaster at a farewell dinner party. What better way to preserve it, and all of the party memories, than in gold?

Materials

- photo
- one 12" x12" (30.5 cm x 30.5 cm) sheet embossed burgundy paper
- one sheet composition gold leaf
- gift card and envelope
- round paper doily, approximately 4½" (11.5 cm) in diameter
- white pencil
- archival-quality adhesive spray

Tools

- metal-edged ruler
- craft knife
- soft paintbrush with a blunt end, such as a stencil brush
- kneaded rubber eraser

Instructions

1. Tear the doily, removing the flat center and one-fourth of the remaining arc. Tear the arc into several sections. Following the manufacturer's directions, lightly coat the front of the doily sections with adhesive spray. Place the gold-leaf paper over the torn sections, and gently press to adhere. With the paintbrush, brush the gold leaf to remove any excess from around the edges and from the recesses of the doily sections.

2. Referring to the photo for placement, set the doily sections on the burgundy paper. Use the pencil to mark lightly the top and the bottom of the doily for placement. Coat the backs of the doily sections with adhesive spray. Press in place.

3. Overlapping the doily sections, place the envelope and the gift card on the burgundy paper. Use the pencil to mark the burgundy paper at the corners of the envelope for placement. Coat the back of the envelope with adhesive spray. Press in place. Coat the back of the greeting card with adhesive spray. Press in place.

4. Using the ruler and knife, trim the photo to 3¼" x 5" (8.5 cm x 12.5 cm). Place the photo 2¼" (6 cm) from the right edge and 2" (5 cm) from the bottom edge of the burgundy paper. Use the pencil to mark the burgundy paper at the corners of the photo for placement. Coat the back of the photo with adhesive spray. Press in place.

5. Write the caption with the white pencil.

6. Use the kneaded rubber eraser to remove all pencil marks.

Then and Now

Squinting at the waves . . . a priceless pastime for generations. A touch of gold brings to mind reflected sunlight.

Materials

- photos
- one 12" x 12" (30.5 cm x 30.5 cm) sheet gray paper
- one 12" x 12" (30.5 cm x 30.5 cm) sheet cream paper
- one sheet composition gold leaf
- three imitation wax seals
- black fine-tip marker
- archival-quality adhesive spray
- double-sided adhesive sheet, such as Peel-N-Stick

Tools

- metal-edged ruler
- craft knife
- tracing paper.
- soft paintbrush with a blunt end, such as a stencil brush
- scissors
- kneaded rubber eraser

Instructions

1. Using the ruler and knife, trim the large photo to 9¹⁄₂" x 6¹⁄₄" (24 cm x 16 cm). Place the photo ³⁄₈" (1 cm) from the right edge and ¹⁄₈" (0.3 cm) from the top edge of the gray paper. Use the pencil to lightly mark the gray paper at the corners of the photo for placement. Following the manufacturer's directions, coat the back of the photo with adhesive spray. Press in place. Trim the small photo to 4¹⁄₂" x 3" (11.5 cm x 7.5 cm). Overlapping the large photo, place the small photo 1¹⁄₄" (3 cm) from the right edge and 3³⁄₄" (9.5 cm) from the bottom edge of the gray paper. Use the pencil to mark the gray paper at the corners of the photo for placement. Coat the back of the photo with adhesive spray. Press in place.

2. Trim the cream paper to 12" x 2¹⁄₂" (30.5 cm x 6.5 cm). Tear the top edge of the cream strip. Place the tracing paper over the bottom 1¹⁄₂" (4 cm) of the cream strip. Lightly coat the exposed area with adhesive spray. Place the gold-leaf paper over the adhesive, and gently press to adhere. Use the paintbrush to remove any excess gold leaf from the torn edge of the strip. Place the strip 1³⁄₈" (3.5 cm) from the bottom edge of the gray paper. Use a pencil to mark the gray paper below the strip for placement. Coat the back of the strip with adhesive spray. Press in place.

3. From the double-sided adhesive sheet, cut three circles slightly smaller in diameter than the wax seals. Peel off the protective paper, and attach the adhesive to the backs of the wax seals. Remove the remaining protective paper from the adhesive circles. Referring to the photo for placement, attach the wax seals to the bottom of the strip.

4. Write the title and captions with the fine-tip marker.

5. Use the kneaded rubber eraser to remove all pencil marks.

recipe
23

Sand Painting

Not many materials can beat colored art sand for interesting visual effects. Its unique texture is fuzzy and shiny at the same time. With the help of double-sided adhesive, the sand is applied in one smooth and solid layer. The fine grains of the sand and the variety of available colors allow for detailed designs. Popular scrapbook themes that can be created with sand include hieroglyphics, geckos, sand dollars, sand castles, and egg timers. Note that sand is abrasive, and shiny photos or papers on a facing page may be scratched.

Sample 1. To make a sandy sun, mark the design on the double-sided adhesive. Cut the design from the sheet, and attach it to the paper.

Sample 3. The finished sand-painted sun warms the page.

Sample 2. Remove the protective paper, one section at a time, and sprinkle the exposed adhesive with the colored sand.

Mayan Bird

Geometric bas-relief designs inspired by the ancients can be recreated with brightly colored sand.

MEXICO

Mark and Adam while
backpacking through
the Yucatan.
El Castillo
and Tulum

Materials

- photos
- one 12" x 12" (30.5 cm x 30.5 cm) sheet blue paper
- art sand in the following colors: orange, turquoise, brown, pink, and navy blue
- 48-point rub-on letters
- black fine-tip marker
- archival-quality adhesive spray
- double-sided adhesive sheet, such as Peel-N-Stick

Tools

- pencil
- tracing paper
- scissors
- craft knife
- metal-edged ruler
- dish towel

Instructions

1. Use the tracing paper to make the border and the bird templates. (See Mayan Border template on page 106 and Mayan Bird template on page 103.) From the double-sided adhesive sheet, cut one border. Use the pencil to lightly mark the blue paper 1 1/8" (3 cm) from the left edge and 2 3/4" (7 cm) from the top edge for border placement. Peel off the protective paper, and attach the border to the blue paper. Remove the remaining protective paper to expose the adhesive. Lightly sprinkle several small areas along the bottom of the border with the turquoise sand. Remove any excess sand. Sprinkle the orange sand over the remaining area of the border. Remove any excess sand.

2. From the double-sided adhesive sheet, cut one bird. Use the pencil to mark the design on the top layer of the protective paper. Place the bird with the tail 1 1/2" (4 cm) from the left edge and the base

5" (12.5 cm) from the top edge of the blue paper. Peel the protective paper from the back of the bird, and, using your marks as guides, attach it to the blue paper. Use the craft knife to cut lightly along the marked lines, being careful to cut through only the protective layer of the adhesive. Remove the protective layer of paper from the wing, the vertical band on the tail, and the base. Sprinkle the turquoise sand over the exposed areas. Remove any excess sand. Continue this process, removing the protective paper for only one color at a time. The eye and beak are navy blue, the body and top tail feather are brown, the head and the bottom tail feather are orange, and the wing feather and the middle tail feather are pink. Gently wipe the blue paper with the dish towel because the rub-on letters and photos won't adhere well if there is any sand residue on the page.

3. Following the manufacturer's directions, apply the rub-on letters. To make the spacing easier, start with the center letter and work out in both directions.

4. Using the ruler and knife, trim the photos to the following sizes, from the top and moving clockwise: 4" x 2 1/2" (10 cm x 6.5 cm), 4 3/4" x 4" (12 cm x 10 cm), 3 3/4" x 2 3/4 (9.5 cm x 7 cm), 4 1/2" x 2 3/4" (11.5 cm x 7 cm), and 4 1/2" x 2 3/4" (11.5 cm x 7 cm). Note the overlaps. Referring to the photo for placement, arrange the photos on the blue paper. Use the pencil to mark the blue paper at the corners of the photos for placement. Following the manufacturer's directions, coat the backs of the photos with adhesive spray. Press in place.

5. Write the captions with the fine-tip marker.

6. Use the kneaded rubber eraser to remove all pencil marks.

Falling Leaves

Falling leaves made from sand can catch the light almost as well as their botanical counterparts.

Materials

- photo
- one 12" x 12" (30.5 cm x 30.5 cm) sheet tan patterned paper
- one 8 1/2" x 11" (21.5 cm x 28 cm) sheet tan vellum
- black photo corners
- brown art sand
- pink art sand
- brown chisel-tip marker
- double-sided adhesive sheet, such as Peel-N-Stick

Tools

- tracing paper
- pencil
- scissors
- craft knife
- metal-edged ruler
- dish towel

Instructions

1. Use the tracing paper to make the leaf template. (See Leaf template on page 104.) From the double-sided adhesive sheet, cut five leaves. Referring to the photo, arrange the leaves in a random pattern around the top and the sides of the tan paper. Use the pencil to mark the tan paper at chosen reference points on the leaves for placement. Peel off the protective paper, and attach the leaves to the tan paper. Remove the remaining protective paper from the leaves to expose the adhesive. Lightly sprinkle the bottom edge of the bottom leaves with the pink sand. Remove any excess sand. Sprinkle the brown sand over all of the leaves. Remove any excess sand. Gently wipe the tan paper with the dish towel because the photo corners won't adhere well if there is any sand residue on the page.

2. From the tan vellum, cut two leaves. Fold the leaves in half, lengthwise. From the double-sided adhesive sheet, cut one leaf. Cut the leaf in half, lengthwise. Peel the protective paper from the back of one half, and attach it to the back of one of the folded leaves. Repeat with the remaining leaf. Use the pencil to mark the tan paper at chosen reference points on the leaves for placement. Remove the remaining protective paper, and press the leaves in place.

3. Using the ruler and knife, trim the photo to 6 1/4" x 4 1/2" (16 cm x 11.5 cm). Place the photo 1 1/2" (4 cm) from the right edge and 3 3/4" (9.5 cm) from the top edge of the tan paper. Use the pencil to mark the tan paper at the corners of the photo for placement. Following the manufacturer's directions, attach the photo to the paper with the photo corners.

4. Write the caption using the chisel-tip marker.

5. Use the kneaded rubber eraser to remove all pencil marks.

Micro Beads

For a unique and shimmery 3-D effect, look to glass micro beads, sometimes called tiny marbles, holeless beads, or no-hole beads. This popular embellishment is easy to apply using strong, double-sided sheets, craft glue, or heat-activated liquid adhesives.

Micro beads work best on pages where you want to achieve a festive, glittery design, such as wedding pages or party and celebration pages. Micro beads are available in a wide array of colors, both single colored and multicolored; pearlescent and metallic finishes; and a number of specials shapes. Just apply the tape in the shape of the desired design, then sprinkle on the beads and gently press. Sprinkle a second time, if needed.

Sample 2. Cut a heart shape from an adhesive sheet. Peel off the protective paper, and attach the heart to the background paper. Using the craft knife, cut a curve through the protective paper only. Remove the paper from the small area to expose the adhesive. Place one large bead on the adhesive, and then fill in with micro beads. Remove the remaining protective paper, and apply multicolored micro beads.

Sample 1. To make a beaded frame, cut strips from an adhesive sheet. Peel off the protective paper, and, overlapping the edge of the photo, attach the strips to the background paper. Remove the remaining protective paper, and apply clear beads to the exposed adhesive.

Sample 3. Create a decorative border to accent initials or a page title. Cut curvy shapes from the adhesive sheet, peel off the protective paper, and position the shapes on the background above and below the lettering. Remove the remaining protective paper, and apply assorted beads on the exposed adhesive.

Friends

Create festive micro-bead borders for a favorite photo. Accent the page further by adding some glistening stars.

Materials

- photo
- one 12" x 12" (30.5 cm x 30.5 cm) sheet pink paper
- one 9" x 12" (23 cm x 30.5 cm) sheet tan vellum
- one 9" x 12" (23 cm x 30.5 cm) sheet cream paper
- purple micro beads, mixed
- double-sided adhesive sheet, such as Peel-N-Stick
- archival-quality adhesive spray

Tools

- craft knife
- metal-edged ruler
- tracing paper
- scissors
- kneaded rubber eraser
- black fine-tip marker (optional)

Instructions

1. Using the ruler and knife, trim the vellum to 8 1/2" x 8 1/2" (21.5 cm x 21.5 cm). Place the trimmed vellum 1 1/8" (3 cm) from the right edge, and 1 3/8" (3.5 cm) from the bottom edge of the pink paper. Use the pencil to lightly mark the pink paper at the corners of the vellum for placement. Following the manufacturer's directions, coat the back of the vellum with adhesive spray. Press in place.

2. Use the marker to print a poem or a personal sentiment on the cream paper (or do this on a computer). Center the poem, and trim the cream paper to 5 1/4" x 6" (13.5 cm x 15 cm). Place the poem box 2 5/8" (6.5 cm) from the right edge and 2" (5 cm) from the bottom edge of the pink paper. Use the pencil to lightly mark the vellum at the corners of the trimmed cream paper for placement. Coat the back of the cream paper with adhesive spray. Press in place.

3. Trim the photo to 4 1/4" x 3 3/4" (11 cm x 9.5 cm). From the double-sided adhesive sheet, cut two 4 1/4" x 1/2" (11 cm x 1 cm) strips. Peel off the protective paper, and attach the adhesive strips to the top and bottom of the photo. Referring to the photo for placement and overlapping the cream paper, place the photo diagonally on the page. Use the pencil to lightly mark the pink paper and the vellum at the corners of the photo for placement. Coat the back of the photo with adhesive spray. Press in place.

4. Photocopy the Star template and use the tracing paper to make the template. From the double-sided adhesive sheet, cut two

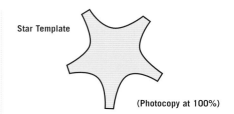

Star Template

(Photocopy at 100%)

stars. Peel off the protective paper, and, referring to the photo for placement, attach the stars to the pink paper.

5. Use the kneaded rubber eraser to remove all pencil marks.

6. Remove the remaining paper from the strips and the stars. Sprinkle the beads on the exposed adhesive. Remove any excess beads. Sprinkle again, if necessary.

Wedding Streamers

Make a dazzling yet elegant wedding layout by adding curving, beaded strips that wind their way off the edges of the page.

Materials

- photos
- one 12" x 12" (30.5 cm x 30.5 cm) straw paper
- silver and white micro beads, mixed
- black photo corners
- double-sided adhesive sheet, such as Peel-N-Stick

Tools

- craft knife
- metal-edged ruler
- tracing paper
- scissors
- pencil
- kneaded rubber eraser

Instructions

1. Using the ruler and knife, trim the photos to 6" x 4½" (15 cm x 11.5 cm). Referring to the photo for placement, set the photos diagonally on the straw paper. Use the pencil to mark lightly the straw paper at the corners of the photos for placement. Slide the photo corners on the photos. Following the manufacturer's directions, attach the photos to the straw paper with the photo corners.

2. Use the kneaded rubber eraser to remove all pencil marks.

3. Use the tracing paper to make the streamer templates. (See Streamers templates on page 108.) From the double-sided adhesive sheet, cut the streamers. Peel off the protective paper; referring to the photo for placement, attach the streamers to the right corner of the straw paper.

4. Remove the remaining protective paper from the streamers. Sprinkle the beads on the exposed adhesive. Remove the excess beads. Sprinkle again, if necessary.

Dip-Dyeing

Dip-dyeing is a simple technique for creating custom-dyed rice papers. To create a sheet of dip-dyed paper, fold a sheet of rice paper, then dip various corners in dyes made from watercolor paint. Open the paper, and let dry. The effect creates a softly mottled background with a lovely texture resulting from the folds. Tearing, rather than cutting, the edges of your rice paper pieces also creates a soft deckle effect.

The sheet can be used whole, or gently torn into smaller pieces that can be used as paper tiles, collage accents, or as background papers.

Sample 1. Originally white paper with gold threads, these pink- and orange-hued pieces of rice paper were dyed following the folding and dipping sequence explained in the first project. Burgundy and gold watercolor paints were used.

Sample 2. This sample, which also started with white rice paper, was created by accordion-folding the paper in two directions and dyeing one edge with lavender watercolor paint. The folds help spread the pigment into the creases.

X-O-X-O

Use a soft lavender dip-dyed paper as the background for a simple page layout that features a lovely black-and-white photo of a happy couple. Write the caption with a lavender pencil to coordinate with the dyed background.

Materials

- photo
- one 12" x 12" (30.5 cm x 30.5 cm) sheet white paper
- one sheet rice paper, available at art supply stores (embedded gold threads optional)
- one 9" x 12" (23 cm x 30.5 cm) sheet cream
- paint
- esive

LEGIS

Tools

- atomizer containing water
- saucer
- paper towels
- scissors
- craft knife
- metal-edged ruler
- pencil

Instructions

1. From the rice paper, cut four 6¹/₂" (16.5 cm) squares. Use the atomizer to slightly mist both sides of each square. Referring to Diagram A, fold the squares. In the saucer, mix the lavender watercolor paint in approximately 6 tablespoons of water. Referring to Diagram B, dip the corners of the folded squares in the paint, allowing the paper to absorb the paint. Unfold the squares, and place them on the paper towels to dry. Do not overlap the squares, and do not blot them because blotting will remove the color.

2. Use the pencil to lightly mark a horizontal and a vertical line in the center of the white paper to divide it into quarters. Carefully tear the edges around each rice paper square. Following the manufacturer's directions, coat the backs of the squares with the adhesive spray. Align one rice paper square in each of the marked squares on the white paper. Press in place.

3. Using the ruler and knife, trim the photo to 6" x 4" (15 cm x 10 cm). Coat the back of the photo with adhesive spray. Place the photo on the cream textured paper, and press to adhere. Allowing ¹/₄" (0.6 cm) around the top and the sides and ³/₄" (2 cm) below the photo, trim the cream paper. Center and place the mounted photo 3¹/₄" (8.5 cm) from top edge of the white paper. Mark the rice paper at the corners of the mounted photo for placement. Coat the back of the mounted photo with adhesive spray. Press in place.

4. Write the names and caption using the purple pencil.

5. Use the kneaded rubber eraser to remove all exposed pencil marks.

Diagram A

Step 1

Step 2

Step 3

Step 4

Diagram B

Dip each corner separately

Vintage Portrait

Use two colors in your dip-dyed paper to echo the muted tones of a vintage photo. You may even want to experiment with coloring your own black-and-white photos to coordinate with your custom dip-dyed papers.

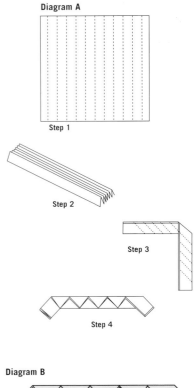

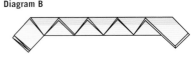

Materials

- photo
- one 12" x 12" (30.5 cm x 30.5 cm) sheet cream paper
- one 9" x 12" (23 cm x 30.5 cm) sheet white paper
- one 9" x 12" (23 cm x 30.5 cm) sheet pink patterned paper
- one sheet rice paper, available at art supply stores (embedded gold threads optional)
- one large bird sticker
- two small rose stickers

- decorative paper border
- gold and burgundy watercolor paint
- archival-quality adhesive spray

Tools

- atomizer containing water
- two saucers
- craft knife
- metal-edged ruler
- pencil
- kneaded rubber eraser
- black fine-tip marker (optional)

Instructions

1. From the rice paper, cut one $11^1/_2$" (29 cm) square. Use the atomizer to slightly mist each side of the rice paper square. Referring to Diagram A, fold the square. In the saucers, mix each color of paint in approximately 6 tablespoons water. Referring to Diagram B, dip the sides of the folded square in the paint, allowing the paper to absorb the paint. Unfold the square, and place it on the paper towel to dry. Do not blot the square because blotting will remove the color.

2. Following the manufacturer's directions, coat the back of the rice paper square with adhesive spray. Center and place the square on the cream paper. Press to adhere. Referring to the photo for placement, attach the stickers to the rice paper. Using the ruler and knife, trim the edge of the overlapping sticker.

3. Using the ruler and knife, trim the photo to 4" x 6" (10 cm x 15 cm). Coat the back of photo with adhesive spray. Place the photo on the white paper, and press to adhere. Center the photo, and trim the white paper to $4^1/_2$" x $6^1/_2$" (11.5 cm x 16.5 cm). Place the mounted photo

$1^3/_8$" (3.5 cm) from the top edge, and $3^3/_4$" (9.5 cm) from the right edge of the cream paper. Use the pencil to mark lightly the rice paper at the corners of the mounted photo for placement. Coat the back of the mounted photo with adhesive spray. Press the mounted photo in place to adhere.

4. Use the marker to print the names and date on the pink patterned paper. Center the names and date, and trim the pink paper to 5" x $1^1/_2$" (12.5 cm x 4 cm). Place the caption box 2" (5 cm) from the right edge and 2" (5 cm) from the bottom edge of the cream paper. Use a pencil to mark the rice paper at the corners of the caption box for placement. Coat the back of the caption box with adhesive spray. Press in place. Trim the two border strips to $2^5/_8$" x $5/_8$" (6.5 cm x 1.5 cm). Coat the backs of the strips with adhesive spray. Center and overlap the strips on the top and bottom edges of the caption box. Press to adhere.

5. Use the kneaded rubber eraser to remove all pencil marks.

Diagram A

Step 1

Step 2

Step 3

Step 4

Diagram B

Aged Paper

The essence of scrapbooking is preserving photos and mementos in a creative and personal fashion. Great care is taken to keep precious memorabilia looking new. Artificially aged paper, however, is the perfect complement to old photos or keepsakes. Old photos and documents are by their nature delicate and fragile, but this delicacy can be highlighted as a design element. Paper can be treated (or mistreated) to simulate aging by wrinkling, sanding, tearing, and painting. These treated papers can then be used as backdrops or accents for the real thing.

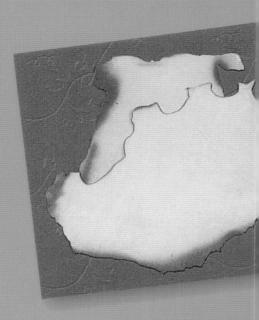

Sample 1. To emphasize wrinkles, crinkle the paper, apply diluted acrylic paint, and dry the paper in a microwave oven to set the wrinkles. Coat the back with adhesive spray. To enhance the three-dimensional effect, compress the paper slightly while pressing it to the page.

Sample 2. Carefully singe the edges of the paper over a candle flame or on a hot stove coil.

Sample 3. To highlight inherent irregularities in handmade paper, lightly coat the paper with spray paint. Let dry, and sand the surface of the paper with fine-grain sandpaper.

Garden Party

This photo and mat board have been naturally aging for the past 90 years, but it took only a few minutes to transform these clip-art flowers from vibrant to vintage.

Materials

- photo
- one 12" x 12" (30.5 cm x 30.5 cm) sheet dark brown paper
- paper flowers cut from color clip art, greeting cards, or wrapping paper
- pages of text
- acrylic sealer
- dark gray acrylic paint
- archival-quality adhesive spray
- double-sided adhesive sheet such as Peel-N-Stick

Tools

- scissors
- sandpaper
- paintbrush
- paper towel
- metal-edged ruler
- craft knife
- kneaded rubber eraser

Instructions

1. From the clip art, cut seven flowers and stems. Apply one coat of sealer to the flowers. Let dry. Repeat with two more coats of sealer. Sand the surface of the flowers in several directions, being careful not to sand completely through the sealer. Dilute the gray acrylic paint to approximately three parts water to one part paint. Paint the flowers with the diluted paint. Blot the paint lightly, leaving some paint in the sanded recesses. Let dry. Repeat painting, if necessary.

2. Tear the pages of text into various lengths and sizes. Following manufacturer's directions, coat the backs of the pages with adhesive spray. Overlapping the pieces, press them in place along the bottom of the sheet of dark brown paper. Using the ruler and knife, trim the overlapping pieces.

3. Referring to the photo for placement, set the flowers around three sides of the brown paper. Use the pencil to lightly mark the brown paper at selected reference points on the flowers for placement. Coat the backs of the flowers. Press the flowers in place to adhere.

4. Referring to the photo for placement, set the photo on the brown paper. Use the pencil to mark the brown paper at the corners of the photo for placement. Cut three strips of double-sided adhesive approximately 1/2" (1 cm) wide. Trim the strips 1/2" (1 cm) shorter than the length of the photo. Peel off the protective paper, and attach the adhesive to the back of the photo. Remove the remaining protective paper, and attach the photo to the page.

5. Use the kneaded rubber eraser to remove all pencil marks.

Letters from France

When are wrinkles attractive? When they complement the age and character of significant treasures.

Materials

- photo
- one 12" x 12" (30.5 cm x 30.5 cm) sheet butterscotch patterned paper
- one 12" x 12" (30.5 cm x 30.5 cm) sheet pale green paper
- small paper memorabilia, such as letters, calendar pages, and maps
- postage stickers
- black fine-tip marker
- archival-quality adhesive spray
- double-sided adhesive sheet, such as Peel-N-Stick

Tools

- metal-edged ruler
- craft knife
- pencil

Instructions

1. Using the ruler and knife, trim the green paper to 11¼" x 2¾" (28.5 cm x 7 cm). Place with the right edge flush and 1" (2.5 cm) from the bottom edge of the butterscotch paper. Use the pencil to mark lightly the butterscotch paper along the top edge of the green paper. Arrange the paper items with their bottom edges overlapping the marked line. Trim the photo to 3¾" x 5¾" (9.5 cm x 14.5 cm). Place the photo 3¾" (9.5 cm) from the right edge and 2⅛" (5.5 cm) from the top edge of the butterscotch paper. Tuck the paper items behind the photo. Use the pencil to mark the butterscotch paper at the corners of the photo and of the paper items for placement. Use adhesive spray to attach lightweight items to the paper. Use the double-sided adhesive sheet to attach thicker or heavier items to the paper. Press in place. Coat the back of the green strip with adhesive spray. Press in place.

2. Place the remaining paper items on the strip. Use the pencil to mark the butterscotch paper at the corners the paper items for placement. Attach the remaining items to the paper.

3. Referring to the photo for placement, attach the stickers.

4. Write the title using the marker.

5. Use the kneaded rubber eraser to remove all pencil marks.

recipe #

27

Stamping

A rubber stamp and an inkpad are the most user-friendly tools available to paper artists. Stamping is versatile and nearly foolproof. With more enthusiasts shopping for more designs, an eclectic array of motifs is available to choose from. And techniques have become increasingly sophisticated. Stamps are now partnered with masks, bleach, pencils, and powders to create elegant paper projects. So avoid the humdrum, and start stamping with style.

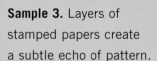

Sample 1. This faded image brings to mind hand-tinted etchings and photographs. After stamping, lightly color in the areas with colored pencils.

Sample 2. Sprinkle metallic embossing powder on wet ink to add some sparkle.

Sample 3. Layers of stamped papers create a subtle echo of pattern.

Little Hands

Stamped images stay within a confined space with the help of a paper stencil.

Materials

- photo
- one 12" x 12" (30.5 cm x 30.5 cm) sheet ivory paper
- one 8¹/₂" x 11" (21.5 cm x 28 cm) sheet cream patterned paper
- one 8¹/₂" x 11" (21.5 cm x 28 cm) sheet melon patterned paper
- one 8¹/₂" x 11" (21.5 cm x 28 cm) sheet light green paper
- one 8¹/₂" x 11" (21.5 cm x 28 cm) sheet light green patterned paper
- one 8¹/₂" x 11" (21.5 cm x 28 cm) sheet tan patterned paper
- one 8¹/₂" x 11" (21.5 cm x 28 cm) sheet typing paper

- alphabet rubber stamps
- 4 to 6 small image rubber stamps
- brown ink
- black ink
- brown pencil
- brown crayon
- archival-quality tape
- archival-quality adhesive spray

Tools

- craft knife
- scissors
- metal-edged ruler
- tracing paper
- pencil
- kneaded rubber eraser

Instructions

1. Use the tracing paper to make the mat template. (See Mat template on page 107.) Cut the photo into an oval shape slightly larger than the window in the template. From the typing paper, make one mat. From the melon patterned paper, cut two mat quadrants. From the cream paper, cut two mat quadrants. Following the manufacturer's directions, coat the backs of the mat quadrants. Place quadrants on the typing paper frame to form a complete oval. Press to adhere. Trim the typing paper, if necessary. Secure the photo to the back of the mat with tape.

2. Referring to the photo for placement, use the brown crayon to trace around the child's hands. Trace over crayon hands on tracing paper, and cut out the centers. Leave the paper around the hands complete to use as a stencil. Align both pairs of hands, and place the stencil on the ivory paper. Use the brown and the black ink to stamp the images in the spaces. Let dry. Remove the stencil.

3. Using the ruler and knife, trim the green patterned paper to 4³/₄" x 2³/₄" (12 cm x 7 cm). Place the green print rectangle diagonally in the top-right corner of the ivory paper, with the left corner 2" (5 cm) and the right corner ¹/₂" (1 cm) from the top edge of the paper. Use the pencil to lightly mark the ivory paper at the corners of the green print rectangle for placement. Coat the back of the rectangle with adhesive spray. Press in place.

4. Referring to the photo for placement and overlapping the rectangle slightly, place the matted photo on the ivory paper. Use the pencil to mark the ivory paper at the top and the bottom of the oval mat for placement. Coat the back of the matted photo with the adhesive spray. Press in place.

5. Trim the cream paper to 11" x 4" (28 cm x 10 cm). Referring to the photo for placement, set the rectangle diagonally on the bottom of the ivory paper, with the top-right corner 4" (10 cm) from the bottom edge of the ivory paper and the top-left corner 1¹/₂" (4 cm) from the bottom edge of the ivory paper. Use the pencil to mark the ivory paper at the top edge of the cream rectangle. Coat the back of the cream rectangle with adhesive spray. Press in place. Use the ruler and the knife to trim the overlapping edges of the cream rectangle.

6. From the tan paper, cut one 6" x 5" x 3³/₈" (15 cm x 12.5 cm x 8.5 cm) triangle. Coat the back of the triangle with adhesive spray. Overlapping the cream rectangle, place the triangle in the bottom-left corner of the ivory paper, and press to adhere. From the green paper, cut one 5³/₄" x 4⁵/₈" x 3" (14.5 cm x 11.5 cm x 7.5 cm) triangle. Coat the back of the triangle with adhesive spray. Place the green triangle on the brown triangle, and press to adhere. From the green patterned paper, cut one 3¹/₄" x 2³/₄" x 4¹/₄" (8.5 cm x 7 cm x 11 cm) triangle. Coat the back of the triangle with adhesive spray. Place the green print triangle in the bottom-right corner, and press to adhere.

7. Use the brown ink to stamp the name on the green print rectangle. Let dry. Use the brown ink to stamp the alphabet on the cream rectangle. Let dry. Use the brown pencil to write caption on the green print rectangle below the stamped name.

8. Use the kneaded rubber eraser to remove all pencil marks.

Golf Heaven

Lift the dye from colored paper with this clever technique. Each solid color of paper produces its own unique reverse-dye color. Swab small sample snippets with bleach to reveal the surprise results.

Materials

- photos
- one 12" x 12" (30.5 cm x 30.5 cm) sheet dark blue patterned paper
- one 12" x 12" (30.5 cm x 30.5 cm) sheet blue paper
- one 8 1/2" x 11" (21.5 cm x 28 cm) sheet maize paper
- one 8 1/2" x 11" (21.5 cm x 28 cm) sheet plum paper
- 48-point rub-on letters
- liquid bleach
- small cosmetic sponges
- brown ink
- sun rubber stamp
- archival-quality adhesive spray

Tools

- scissors
- small saucer
- paper towel
- craft knife
- metal-edged ruler
- pencil
- kneaded rubber eraser

Instructions

1. From the cosmetic sponges, cut two or three cloud shapes measuring approximately 2" x 1" (5 cm x 2.5 cm). Tear several layers of paper towel, and place them in the saucer. Pour enough bleach into the saucer to saturate the paper towels. Dip the cloud sponges in the bleach, and stamp the top edge of the blue paper, overlapping shapes, if desired. Let dry. Note: Immediately after stamping, rinse the sponges and the rubber stamp thoroughly with running water. Continued exposure to the bleach will corrode them. Dip the sun stamp in the bleach, and stamp the top edge of the maize paper. Let dry. Rinse the stamp thoroughly with running water. Use the brown ink to stamp the top edge of the maize paper over the beached sun. Let dry.

2. Tear a 2 1/2" (6.5 cm)-wide strip from the blue paper. Make sure to include the bleached clouds in the section that you tear. Following the manufacturer's directions, coat the back of the strip with adhesive spray. Place the strip 1/4" (0.6 cm) from the top edge of the dark blue patterned paper. Press in place. Tear around the sides and bottom of sun, measuring 3 1/2" x 2 1/2" (9 cm x 6.5 cm). Consider the locations of the clouds on the blue strip, and place the sun rectangle on top of the cloud strip. Use the pencil to lightly mark the dark blue paper at the corners of the sun rectangle for placement. Coat the back of the sun rectangle with adhesive spray. Press in place.

3. Using the ruler and knife, trim the photos to the following sizes, clockwise from left: 6" x 4" (15 cm x 10 cm), 3 1/2" x 4 1/2" (9 cm x 11.5 cm), and 3 1/4" x 5 1/2" (8.5 cm x 14 cm). Referring to the photo for placement, arrange the photos on the dark blue paper with the top-right photo overlapping the cloud strip. Use the pencil to mark lightly the dark blue paper and the cloud strip at the corners of the photos for placement. Coat the backs of the photos with the adhesive spray. Press the photos in place.

4. Trim the plum paper to 6" x 1 3/8" (15 cm x 3.5 cm). Using the ruler and pencil, lightly draw a baseline for rub-on letters. Following the manufacturer's directions and using the marked line as a guide, apply the rub-on letters. To make the spacing easier, start with the center letters and work out in both directions. Place the title strip on the dark blue paper with the top edge of the strip 1/4" (0.6 cm) from the bottom edge of the left photo. Use the pencil to mark the dark blue paper at the corners of the strip for placement. Coat the back of the strip with adhesive spray. Press in place.

5. Use the kneaded rubber eraser to remove all pencil marks.

Decoupage

Although this technique was developed in Venice, its name is derived from a French word, *découper*, which means "to cut out." Decoupage is a creative, step-by-step process of cutting, pasting, and varnishing. European artists used this process to transform plain surfaces to look as though they had been hand-painted. The traditional treatment has been simplified for scrapbook art. Because this adaptation requires no intricate cutting, it is actually decoupage without the découper. The varnishing is done with ordinary craft glue.

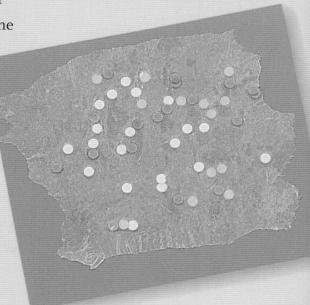

Sample 1. Use this technique to embed confetti in a paper appliqué. Place the confetti on plastic wrap, and cover it with a single layer of tissue.

Sample 2. Carefully coat the tissue with a layer of diluted white craft glue, and let dry. Repeat with a second coat of glue.

Sample 3. Carefully peel the tissue from the plastic wrap, and trim it into a fun shape. Attach it to the page with adhesive spray.

Yankee Doodle Dandies

Transform bright paper napkins into opaque paper appliqués.

Materials

- photos
- one 12" x 12" (30.5 cm x 30.5 cm) sheet white paper
- one 8 1/2" x 11" (21.5 cm x 28 cm) sheet of each of six different shades of blue paper
- one 8 1/2" x 11" (21.5 cm x 28 cm) sheet of yellow paper
- printed napkins
- blue pencil
- black fine-tip marker
- white craft glue
- archival-quality adhesive spray

Tools

- metal-edged ruler
- craft knife
- pencil
- curved-corner paper punch
- plastic wrap
- paintbrush
- kneaded rubber eraser

Instructions

1. Remove and discard the bottom ply from the print napkins. Tear three 4" (10 cm) squares from the napkins. Dilute the craft glue to approximately two parts water to one part glue. Place the torn squares on the plastic wrap. Use the paintbrush to carefully paint one coat of the diluted glue into the squares. Let dry. Repeat with one more coat of glue.

2. Use the pencil to draw light horizontal and vertical lines spaced 3" (7.5 cm) apart on the white paper. Using the ruler and the knife, cut one 5 7/8" (15 cm) square from one sheet of blue paper. From each of the remaining blue papers, cut one 2 7/8" (7.5 cm) square. From the yellow paper, cut one 2 7/8" (7.5 cm) square. Referring to the photo for placement, set the colored squares on the corresponding white squares. Following the manufacturer's directions, coat the backs of the squares with the adhesive spray. Press the squares in place to adhere. Trim the coated napkin squares to 2 7/8" (7.5 cm) squares. Place the napkin squares on the corresponding white squares. Coat the backs of the napkin squares with adhesive spray. Press the squares in place.

3. Trim the large photo to 4 3/8" x 4" (11 cm x 10 cm). Use the corner punch to punch the corners of the photo. Place the photo in the center of the large blue square. Use the pencil to mark the blue paper at the corners of the photo for placement. Coat the back of the photo with adhesive spray. Press in place. Trim the small photo to a 2 7/8" (7.5 cm) square. Coat the back of the photo with adhesive spray. Place in the corresponding square, and press to adhere.

4. Use the pencil and the ruler to draw light horizontal lines in the top white square to use as a baseline for the title. Use the blue pencil to write the title. Write the captions for the photos using the fine-tip marker.

5. Use the kneaded rubber eraser to remove all pencil marks.

Wedding Wreath

Theses delicate tissue blossoms and berries weren't hand-painted, although they look as if they were. This labor of love took almost no time at all to complete.

Materials

- photos
- one 12" x 12" (30.5 cm x 30.5 cm) sheet white enamel finish paper
- one 12" x 12" (30.5 cm x 30.5 cm) sheet pale green paper
- printed napkins
- black fine-tip marker
- white craft glue
- archival-quality adhesive spray

Tools

- metal-edged ruler
- craft knife
- pencil
- plastic wrap
- paintbrush
- kneaded rubber eraser

Instructions

1. Remove and discard the bottom ply from the printed napkins. Tear 12 to 15 small images from the napkins. Dilute the craft glue to approximately two parts water to one part glue. Place the torn squares on the plastic wrap. Use the paintbrush to carefully paint the squares with one coat of diluted glue. Let dry. Repeat with one more coat of glue.

2. Using the ruler and knife, trim the photo to 3$\frac{1}{2}$" x 5$\frac{1}{4}$" (9 cm x 13.5 cm). Place the photo 3$\frac{1}{4}$" (8.5 cm) from the left edge and 2" (5 cm) from the top edge of the white paper. Use the pencil to lightly mark the white paper at the corners of the photo for placement. Trim the green paper to 2$\frac{1}{4}$" x 12" (6 cm x 30.5 cm). Align the green strip with the right edge of the white paper. Use the pencil to mark the white paper along the left edge of the green strip for placement. Following the manufacturer's directions, coat the back of the photo and of the strip with adhesive spray. Press in place.

3. Referring to the photo for placement, arrange the images around the photo. Use the pencil to mark the white paper at the top and bottom of each image for placement. Coat the backs of the images with the adhesive spray. Press in place.

4. Write the title using the fine-tip marker.

5. Use the kneaded rubber eraser to remove all pencil marks.

Marbling

Marbled paper is characterized by flowing, organic patterns that resemble ocean waves or striated rock. It is reproduced commercially for use as end papers and as wallpaper. To marble paper, colors are floated on a surface of thickened liquid. The colors can be manipulated to form specific patterns or left untouched to spread and co-mingle naturally. The paper is placed face-down on the surface to transfer the design. It is an instant-gratification art because the design appears as soon as the paper touches the paint. Like snowflakes, each individual print is unique.

Beginning marbling can be done on a gelatin surface. Simply drop the paint on the set gelatin, and let it spread. Then print. The sugar in the gelatin actually leaves a nice glaze on the paper. Then try floating the paint on a less stable surface, such as liquid starch or commercially prepared solutions such as carrageen. Liquid surfaces allow for more design variation. Remember to discard the gelatin after use.

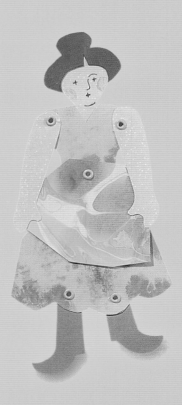

Sample 1. Dress a paper doll in bold marbled papers. The doll's apron was made from paper that was marbled with liquid starch.

Sample 2. Make a declarative statement on a colorful and campy backdrop.

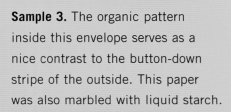

Sample 3. The organic pattern inside this envelope serves as a nice contrast to the button-down stripe of the outside. This paper was also marbled with liquid starch.

You're Out of This World

For stellar results, keep silhouettes simple when working with fancy paper.

Materials

- photo
- one 12" x 12" (30.5 cm x 30.5 cm) sheet black paper
- one 8$\frac{1}{2}$" x 11" (21.5 cm x 28 cm) sheet blue paper
- one 8$\frac{1}{2}$" x 11" (21.5 cm x 28 cm) sheet cream paper
- acrylic paint in the following colors: red, gray, gold, and blue (or alternate colors)
- gelatin
- white milky pen
- archival-quality adhesive spray

Tools

- 9" x 12" (23 cm x 30.5 cm) glass or metal tray
- eye droppers (optional)
- feather or fork (optional)
- old newspaper torn into 3" (7.5 cm)-wide strips
- paper towel
- iron
- tracing paper
- scissors
- craft knife
- metal-edged ruler
- curved-corner paper punch
- kneaded rubber eraser

Instructions

1. Following the manufacturer's directions, make the gelatin, and pour it into the pan. Allow it to set. Dilute each color of paint to approximately three parts water to one part paint. Use either eye droppers or plastic squirt bottles to drop a few drops of each selected color on the surface of the gelatin. Manipulate the paint with the feather or the fork, or let the colors spread naturally. Carefully place the blue paper on the gelatin. Remove the paper from the gelatin. Place the paper on the paper towel. With the newspaper strips, squeegee the excess gelatin from the paper. Let dry. Repeat with the cream paper.

2. Press the paper with an iron to flatten.

3. Use the tracing paper to make the star and planet templates. (See Star and Planet templates on page 109.) Cut the shapes from the corresponding colors. Referring to the photo for placement, set the stars and the planet on the black paper. Place the ring to overlap the right edge of the paper. Use the pencil to lightly mark the black paper at selected reference points on the planet and the stars for placement. Following the manufacturer's directions, coat the backs of the planet and the stars with adhesive. Press them in place. Use the ruler and knife to trim the overlapping piece.

4. Trim the photo to 3$\frac{1}{4}$" x 3$\frac{5}{8}$" (8.3 cm x 9.2 cm). Using the corner punch, punch the corners of the photo. Referring to the photo for placement, set the photo on the black paper. Use the pencil to mark the black paper at the corners of the photo for placement. Coat the back of the photo with the adhesive spray. Press the photo in place to adhere.

5. Write the title and the caption using the milky pen.

6. Use the kneaded rubber eraser to remove all pencil marks.

A Windy Day

Patchwork kites made from marbled paper are a high-flying success.

Materials

- photo
- one 12" x 12" (30.5 cm x 30.5 cm) sheet blue paper
- one 8 1/2" x 11" (21.5 cm x 28 cm) sheet blue paper
- one 8 1/2" x 11" (21.5 cm x 28 cm) sheet cream paper
- one 8 1/2" x 11" (21.5 cm x 28 cm) sheet yellow paper
- one 8 1/2" x 11" (21.5 cm x 28 cm) sheet black paper
- blue print fabric
- alphabet stamps
- gelatin
- acrylic paint in the following colors; red, gray, gold, and blue (or alternate colors)
- blue ink
- archival-quality adhesive spray
- double-sided adhesive sheet, such as Peel-N-Stick

Tools

- 9" x 12" (23 cm x 30.5 cm) glass or metal tray
- eye droppers (optional)
- feather or fork (optional)
- old newspaper torn into 3" (7.5 cm)-wide strips
- paper towel
- iron
- tracing paper
- scissors
- craft knife
- metal-edged ruler
- kneaded rubber eraser

Instructions

1. Following the manufacturer's directions make the gelatin, and pour it into the pan. Allow it to set. Dilute each color of paint to approximately three parts water to one part paint. Use either eye droppers or plastic squirt bottles to drop a few drops of each selected color on the surface of the gelatin. Manipulate the paint with the feather or the fork, or let the colors spread naturally. Carefully place the blue paper on the gelatin. Remove the paper from the gelatin. Place the paper on the paper towel. With the newspaper strips, squeegee the excess gelatin from the paper. Let dry. Repeat with the cream paper and with the yellow paper.

2. Press the paper with the iron to flatten.

3. Use the tracing paper to make the kite template. (See Kite template on page 109.) Cut one kite from each color. Using the ruler and knife, cut each kite into four sections. Referring to the photo for placement, set the kites on the blue paper. Place the center kite to overlap the top edge of the paper. Use the pencil to lightly mark the blue paper at the corners of the kites for placement. Following the manufacturer's directions, coat the backs of the kite sections with adhesive spray. Press the sections in place. Using the ruler and knife, trim the overlapping pieces.

4. From the black paper, cut one 1/8" x 7 1/2" (0.3 cm x 19 cm) strip. Place the strip below the right kite and 1 3/4" (4.5 cm) from the right edge of the blue paper. Use the pencil to mark the blue paper along the edge of the strip for placement. From the blue fabric cut four 3/8" x 3 1/2" (1 cm x 9 cm) strips. Tie each strip around the black paper strip. From the double-sided adhesive, cut five 1/8" x 1/2" (0.3 cm x 1 cm) strips. Peel off the protective paper, and attach the adhesive to the back of the black paper strip at the top and bottom and between the ties.

Remove the remaining protective paper, and attach the strip to the blue paper. From the double-sided adhesive sheet, cut eight 1/4" (0.6 cm) squares. Peel off the protective paper, and attach the adhesive to the backs of the ties. Remove the remaining protective paper, and attach the ties to the blue paper. Trim the ends of the ties, if necessary.

5. Using the ruler and knife, trim the photo to 5" x 7" (12.5 cm x 18 cm). Place the photo 2 1/2" (6.5 cm) from the left edge and 3/8" (1 cm) from the bottom edge of the blue paper. Use the pencil to mark the blue paper at the corners of the photo for placement. Coat the back of the photo with adhesive spray. Press the photo in place.

6. Use the blue ink to stamp the title above the photo.

7. Use the kneaded rubber eraser to remove all pencil marks.

Mosaics

For centuries, individual tiles, bits of glass, and even small pebbles have been arranged to portray still lifes, landscapes, and borders. Mosaics made from glass and ceramic tile are durable enough to walk on, but mosaics made from craft foam and corrugated paper are lightweight enough to decorate a page. These mosaics have an intriguing, touchable quality, and they are fun to make.

Sample 1. Begin by transferring the line art to the backing paper.

Sample 2. Cut out the silhouette, and attach it to the page over the line art.

Sample 3. Fill in the spaces with paper shapes and corrugated paper tiles.

Teacher Tribute

A drawing is worth a thousand words. These small mosaic flowers are sprinkled on a well-deserved thank-you for a favorite teacher.

Materials

- artwork
- photo
- one 12" x 12" (30.5 cm x 30.5 cm) sheet purple paper
- one 8 1/2" x 11" (21.5 cm x 28 cm) sheet lavender patterned paper
- one 8 1/2" x 11" (21.5 cm x 28 cm) sheet burgundy paper
- 1/16" (0.2 cm) craft foam in light blue, purple, peach, tangerine, yellow, and pink.
- double-sided adhesive sheet, such as Peel-N-Stick
- archival-quality adhesive spray
- archival-quality tape

Tools

- tracing paper
- scissors
- metal-edged ruler
- pencil
- kneaded rubber eraser

Instructions

1. Use the tracing paper to make the flower template. From the double-sided adhesive sheet, cut three flowers. Peel off the protective paper, and, allowing 1/2" (1 cm) between shapes, attach the adhesive to the burgundy paper. Remove the remaining protective paper to expose the adhesive. From the purple craft foam, cut two circles for the flower centers. From the light blue craft foam, cut one circle for the flower center. Place the circles on the adhesive in the centers of the flowers. Cut the remaining colors of foam into small tiles of various shapes. The tiles should range in size from 1/4" (0.6 cm) to 3/8" (1 cm). Working from the center out, carefully pick up each tile with the point of the craft knife, and place it on the adhesive. Refer to the photo for color shading. Leave enough space between each tile for the burgundy paper to show. Outer tiles may need to be trimmed slightly to conform to the curves of the flower petals.

2. Trim each flower, allowing 1/8" (0.3 cm) of paper around outside edge.

3. Using the ruler and the knife, trim the artwork to 8 1/2" x 11" (21.5 cm x 28 cm). Place the artwork 1/4" (0.6 cm) from the right edge and 3/4" (2 cm) from the top edge of the purple paper. Use the pencil to lightly mark the purple paper at the corners of the artwork for placement. Following the manufacturer's directions, coat the back of the artwork with adhesive spray. Press in place.

4. Trim the photo to 2 1/4" x 3" (6 cm x 7.5 cm). Trim the lavender patterned paper to 2 3/4" x 3 1/2" (7 cm x 9 cm). Center and cut a 1 7/8" x 2 5/8" (5 cm x 6.5 cm) window in the lavender rectangle to make a mat. Secure the photo to the back of the mat using the archival-quality tape. Overlapping the artwork, place the matted photo on the purple paper. Use the pencil to mark the purple paper and the artwork

at the corners of the matted photo for placement. Coat the back of the matted photo with adhesive spray. Press in place.

5. Place the mosaic flowers on the paper at chosen spots. Use the pencil to mark the purple paper and the artwork at the flower tops for placement. Coat the backs of the mosaic flowers with adhesive spray. Press the flowers in place.

6. Use the kneaded rubber eraser to remove all pencil marks.

Small Flower Template

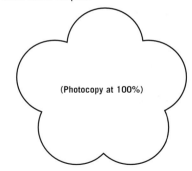

(Photocopy at 100%)

Waves

The movement of watery ocean waves is portrayed with three-dimensional foam tiles. You can almost feel heat of the sun and taste the salty spray of the sea.

Materials

- photos
- one 12" x 12" (30.5 cm x 30.5 cm) sheet shaded pastel paper
- one 8¹/₂" x 11" (21.5 cm x 28 cm) sheet yellow patterned paper
- one 8¹/₂" x 11" (21.5 cm x 28 cm) sheet gold print paper
- ¹/₁₆" (0.2 cm) light blue craft foam
- ¹/₁₆" (0.2 cm) lavender craft foam
- black fine-tip marker
- double-sided adhesive sheet, such as Peel-N-Stick
- archival-quality adhesive spray
- archival-quality tape

Tools

- craft knife
- metal-edged ruler
- scissors
- tracing paper
- pencil
- kneaded rubber eraser

Instructions

1. Using the ruler and knife, trim the yellow patterned paper to 9" x 5" (23 cm x 12.5 cm). Cut a 6¹/₂" x 4¹/₂" (16.5 cm x 11.5 cm) window offset to the right of the rectangle, to make a mat. Trim the large photo to 7" x 5" (18 cm x 12.5 cm). Secure the photo to the back of the mat using the tape. Place the matted photo diagonally on the pastel paper with the left corner 2" (5 cm) and the right corner ¹/₂" (1 cm) from the top edge of the paper. Use the pencil to mark lightly the pastel paper at the corners of the matted photo for placement. Following the manufacturer's directions, coat the back of the matted photo with adhesive spray. Press in place.

2. Trim the gold patterned paper to 8³/₄" x 3¹/₄" (22 cm x 8.5 cm). Center and cut three 2¹/₄" (6 cm) squares in the rectangle to make a mat. Trim the small photos to 2¹/₂" (6.5 cm) squares. Secure the photos to the back of the mat with tape. Place the matted photos diagonally on the pastel paper with the left corner 1" (2.5 cm) and the right corner ¹/₂" (1 cm) from the bottom edge of the paper. Use the pencil to mark the pastel paper at the corners of the matted photo for placement. Coat the back of the matted photo with the adhesive spray. Press in place.

3. Use the tracing paper to make the wave templates. (See Waves templates on page 105.) From the double-sided adhesive sheet, cut one of each wave shape. Referring to the photo for placement, peel the protective paper from the backs of the wave shapes, and attach them to the pastel paper. Remove the remaining protective paper to expose the adhesive. From the blue craft foam, cut one large wave shape. Press it in place on a matching adhesive shape. Cut the lavender and the blue foam into small tiles of various shapes. Tiles should range in size from ¹/₄" (0.6 cm) to ³/₈" (1 cm). Carefully pick up each tile with point of craft knife, and place it on the remaining wave shapes. Refer to the photo for color shading. Leave enough space between each tile so that the pastel paper shows.

4. Write the caption and the names using the fine-tip marker.

5. Use the kneaded rubber eraser to remove all pencil marks.

Layered Borders

Scrapbook enthusiasts of all skill levels know that the easiest solution to a successful page layout is an attention-grabbing border. You can't go wrong with a strong focal point in the center and an interesting graphic along the vertical margin. Build these snappy borders by layering simple geometric strips along the side of the page. No special skills are required—just elementary cutting and gluing.

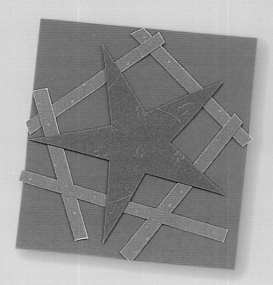

Sample 1. To layer shapes, attach the first layer of the design with double-sided adhesive or adhesive spray.

Sample 2. Attach the second layer of shapes.

Sample 3. Attach the accents to complete the design.

Nick

This basic border sports paper buttons of various colors and sizes. It can be adapted to resemble train tracks or a baby's growth chart.

Materials

- photos
- one 12" x 12" (30.5 cm x 30.5 cm) sheet green paper
- one 12" x 12" (30.5 cm x 30.5 cm) sheet light blue paper
- one 12" x 12" (30.5 cm x 30.5 cm) sheet cream paper
- one 8 1/2" x 11" (21.5 cm x 28 cm) sheet cream paper
- one 8 1/2" x 11" (21.5 cm x 28 cm) sheet cream patterned paper
- one 8 1/2" x 11" (21.5 cm x 28 cm) sheet medium blue paper
- paper buttons in assorted sizes and colors
- archival-quality adhesive spray
- archival-quality tape
- double-sided adhesive sheet

Tools

- craft knife
- metal-edged ruler
- pencil
- scissors
- kneaded rubber eraser

Instructions

1. Using the ruler and knife, cut a 1 3/8" x 12" (3.5 cm x 30.5 cm) strip from the light blue paper. Center and cut twelve 3/4" (2 cm) squares in the strip to make a ladder. From the ivory paper, cut one 1/4" x 12" (0.6 cm x 30.5 cm) strip. Weave the ivory strip through the center of the ladder. From the cream paper, cut three 1" (2.5 cm) squares. From the cream patterned paper, cut three 1" (2.5 cm) squares. Referring to the photo for sequence, tape the squares to the back of the ladder.

2. Place the ladder strip 1 1/4" (3 cm) from the right edge of the green paper. Use the pencil to lightly mark the green paper at the edge of the strip for placement. Following the manufacturer's directions, coat the back of the strip with adhesive spray. Press in place.

3. Referring to the photo for placement, set the buttons on the strip and on the green paper. From the double-sided adhesive sheet, cut circles slightly smaller in diameter than the paper buttons. Peel off the protective paper, and attach adhesive to the backs of the buttons. Remove the remaining protective paper, and attach the buttons to the strip and to the green paper.

4. Trim the photos to 4" x 6" (10 cm x 15 cm). Place the top photo 2 3/4" (7 cm) from the right edge and 1/2" (1 cm) from the top edge of the green paper. Place the bottom photo 2 3/4" (7 cm) from the right edge and 1 1/4" (3 cm) from the bottom edge of the green paper. Use the pencil to mark the green paper at the corners of the photos for placement. Coat the backs of the photos with adhesive spray. Press in place.

5. Use the pencil to draw the letters for the name on the blue paper, making uppercase letters and lowercase letters. Cut the letters for the name from the medium blue paper. Referring to the photo for placement, set the letters on the green paper. Use the pencil to mark the green paper at the top and bottom of each letter for placement. From the double-sided adhesive sheet, cut strips the same width as the letters. Trim the strips to fit the backs of the letters. Peel off the protective paper, and attach the adhesive to the backs of the letters. Remove the remaining protective paper, and press the letters in place.

6. Use the kneaded rubber eraser to remove all pencil marks.

Play Ball

Combining two strands of rickrack to look like a complex braid is an old sewing trick that works even better with paper. By using narrow zigzag strips, a keyhole design appears.

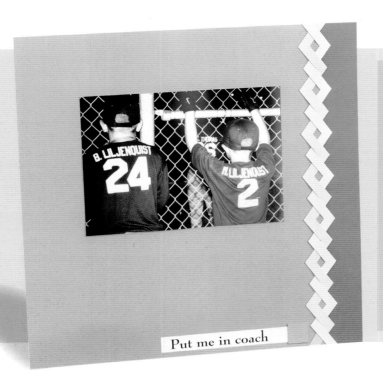

Put me in coach

Materials

- photo
- one 12" x 12" (30.5 cm x 30.5 cm) sheet blue paper
- one 12" x 12" (30.5 cm x 30.5 cm) sheet ivory paper
- one 12" x 12" (30.5 cm x 30.5 cm) sheet light green paper
- one 12" x 12" (30.5 cm x 30.5 cm) sheet rust paper
- one 8½" x 11" (21.5 cm x 28 cm) sheet white paper
- one 8½" x 11" (21.5 cm x 28 cm) sheet medium blue paper
- archival-quality adhesive spray
- archival-quality tape

Tools

- metal-edged ruler
- craft knife
- tracing paper
- scissors
- pencil
- kneaded rubber eraser

Instructions

1. Using the ruler and knife, trim the photo to 5" x 7" (12.5 cm x 18 cm). Place the photo 2¾" (7 cm) from the right edge and 2⅛" (5.5 cm) from the top edge of the blue paper. Use the pencil to lightly mark the blue paper at the corners of the photo for placement. Following the manufacturer's directions, coat the back of the photo with adhesive spray. Press in place.

2. Trim the rust paper to 1¼" x 12" (3 cm x 30.5 cm). Coat the back of the strip with the adhesive spray. Align the top, the bottom, and the right edge of the strip with the blue paper, and press in place.

3. Use the tracing paper to make the zigzag template. (See Long Zag template on page 104.) Cut one zigzag strip from both the ivory paper and the light green paper. Hold the strips so that they are mirror images of each other, and wrap them around each other so that they are intertwined from the top to the bottom of the strips. Referring to the photo, pull the strips apart enough to create negative spaces. Coat the back of the strip with adhesive spray. Press in place to cover the left edge of the rust strip.

4. Use the pencil to print the title on the white paper. Trim the title box to 4¾" x ⅝" (12 cm x 1.5 cm). Place the title box 2½" (6.5 cm) from the right edge and ⅛" (0.3 cm) from the bottom edge of the blue paper. Use the pencil to mark the blue paper at the corners of the title box for placement. Coat the back of the title box with adhesive spray. Press in place. From the medium blue paper, cut one ¾" (1.9 cm) square. Coat the back of the square with adhesive spray, and press in place over the right end of the title box.

5. Use the kneaded rubber eraser to remove all pencil marks.

Tassels

Tassels have a modest beginning as loose threads, knotted together to prevent coarse fabrics from unraveling. Over the years they evolved into lovely, frivolous objects that decorate pillows and window shades. Tassels used for textile embellishment are borrowed to serve as exotic additions to these paper projects. They are made from ordinary cotton floss that is wrapped, knotted, and snipped to make swingy pendants.

Sample 1. Adorn a plain paper cuff with a bright cotton tassel.

Sample 2. No mortarboard is complete without a swinging tassel.

Sample 3. Brighten up a dreary page with a tassel-trimmed umbrella.

Old-World Christmas Tree

Reminisce about romantic and formal Christmas scenes with a few well-placed tassels.

Materials

- photos
- one 12" x 12" (30.5 cm x 30.5 cm) sheet taupe patterned paper
- one 8½" 11 (21.5 cm x 28 cm) sheet green paper
- one 8½" x 11" (21.5 cm x 28 cm) sheet gold-striped paper
- gold pearl cotton, size 5
- brown paper bow
- alphabet stickers
- archival-quality adhesive spray
- archival-quality tape

Tools

- metal-edged ruler
- craft knife
- chipboard
- scissors
- pencil
- tracing paper
- round hole punch, ⅛" (0.3 cm) in diameter
- kneaded rubber eraser

Instructions

1. Using the ruler and knife, trim the top photos to 3¼" (8.5 cm) squares. Trim the bottom photo to 4" x 5¼" (10 cm x 13.5 cm). Following the manufacturer's directions, coat the back of the bottom photo with adhesive spray. Place the photo on the gold-striped paper, and press. Center the photo and trim the gold-striped paper to 4½" x 5¾" (11.5 cm x 14.5 cm).

2. Place the top photo 1⅝" (4 cm) from the right edge and ¼" (0.6 cm) from the top edge of the taupe paper. Overlapping the corner of the top photo, place the middle photo 4" (10 cm) from the right edge and 2½" (6.5 cm) from the top edge of the taupe paper. Place the mounted photo 1⅞" (5 cm) from the left edge and ¼" (0.6 cm) from the bottom edge of the taupe paper. Mark the taupe paper at the corners of the photos for placement. Coat the backs of the photos with adhesive spray. Press them in place.

3. From the chipboard, cut one 3" x 1¾" (7.5 cm x 4.5 cm) rectangle. Wrap the pearl cotton around the short length of the rectangle 18 to 20 times. Cut two 5" (12.5 cm) lengths of pearl cotton. Thread one length under the wrapped pearl cotton, and knot at the top edge of the chipboard. Slide the wrapped pearl cotton from the chipboard. Referring to Diagram A, wrap the second length around the top of the wrapped bundle, and knot to secure. Trim the ends. Cut through the loops at the bottom of the bundle to create a tassel. Repeat to make four more tassels.

4. Use the tracing paper to make the Christmas tree template. (See Christmas Tree template on page 108.) From the green paper, cut one Christmas tree. Punch holes in the tree, where indicated. Thread the tassel ties through each hole, and secure the ties to the back of the tree with the tape. Coat the back of the tree with adhesive spray. Align the right edge of the tree with the right edge of the taupe paper. Press in place. Coat the back of the paper bow with adhesive spray. Center along the bottom of the trunk and press in place.

5. Attach the stickers to taupe paper.

6. Use the kneaded rubber eraser to remove all pencil marks.

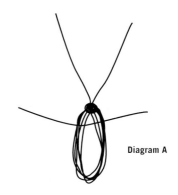

Diagram A

Lunatic Fringe

This row of dancing tassels brings to mind fun combined with fashion.

Materials

- photo
- one 12" x 12" (30.5 cm x 30.5 cm) sheet dark blue paper
- one 8½" x 11" (21.5 cm x 28 cm) sheet pink patterned paper
- party invitation
- paper tag with string
- paper button
- blue plastic nails for paper
- size 5 pearl cotton in variegated pink, variegated purple, variegated turquoise, and solid pink
- black fine-tip marker
- archival-quality adhesive spray

Tools

- metal-edged ruler
- craft knife
- chipboard
- scissors
- pencil
- kneaded rubber eraser

Instructions

1. Using the ruler and knife, trim the photo to 4" x 6" (10 cm x 15 cm). Place the photo 1⅞" (5 cm) from the right edge and 1¾" (4.4 cm) from the top edge of the blue paper. Use the pencil to lightly mark the blue paper at the corners of the photo for placement. Following the manufacturer's directions, coat the back of the photo with adhesive spray. Press in place. Referring to the photo for placement, set the invitation diagonally on the blue paper with the left corner 1¼" (3 cm) and the right corner ¾" (2 cm) from the top edge of the blue paper. Mark the blue paper at the corners of the invitation for placement. Coat the back of the invitation with adhesive spray. Coat the back of the paper button with adhesive spray. Press in place on blue paper, overlapping the top edge of the invitation. Coat the back of the tag with adhesive spray. Press in place on blue paper, overlapping left edge of invitation.

2. From the chipboard, cut one 3" x 1¾" (7.5 cm x 4.5 cm) rectangle. Wrap the variegated pink pearl cotton around the short length of the rectangle 18 to 20 times. Cut two 5" (12.5 cm) lengths of variegated pink pearl cotton. Thread one length under the wrapped pearl cotton, and knot at the top edge of the chipboard. Slide the wrapped pearl cotton from the chipboard. Referring to Diagram A, wrap the second length around the top of the wrapped bundle, and knot to secure. Trim the ends. Cut through the loops at the bottom of the bundle to create a tassel. Repeat to make one more variegated pink tassel, three variegated purple tassels, one variegated turquoise tassel, and one solid pink tassel.

3. From the pink patterned paper, cut one 11" x ⅝" (28 cm x 1.5 cm) strip. Center and place the strip 3¼" (8.5 cm) from the bottom edge of the blue paper. Mark the blue paper at the ends of the strip for placement. Trim the ends of the tassels as desired. Referring to the photo for placement, set the tassels in a horizontal row on the blue paper. Coat the back of the pink print strip with adhesive spray. Press in place over the tassel ties to adhere. Use the craft knife to cut small holes in the strip at each end and between tassels. Following the manufacturer's directions, insert nails in the holes and secure.

4. Write the caption on the tag using the fine-tip marker.

5. Use the kneaded rubber eraser to remove all pencil marks.

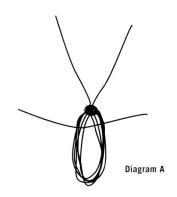

Diagram A

templates

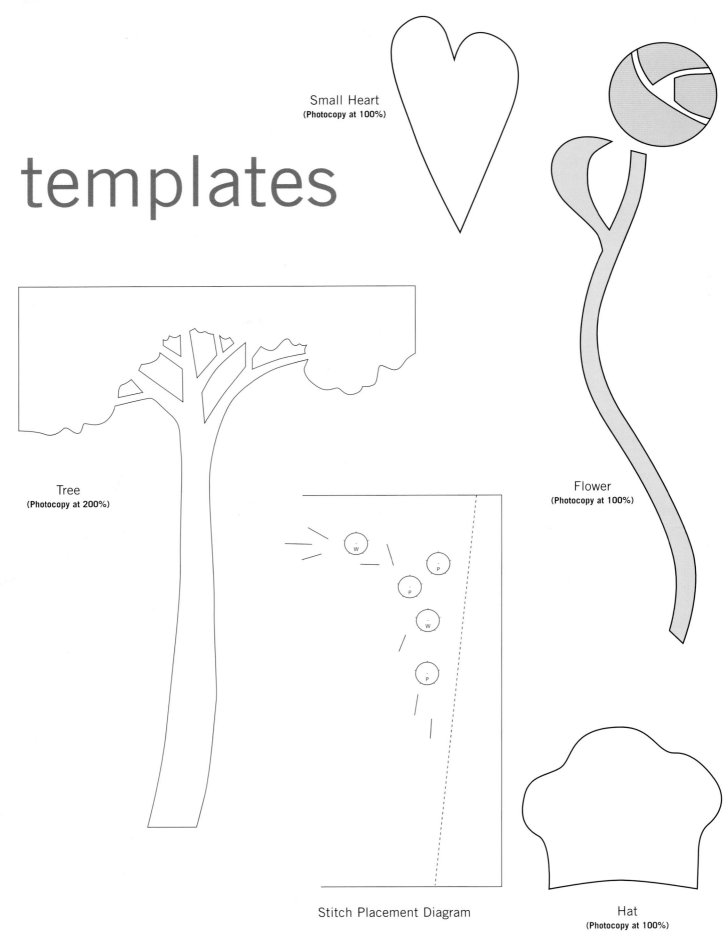

Small Heart
(Photocopy at 100%)

Tree
(Photocopy at 200%)

Flower
(Photocopy at 100%)

Stitch Placement Diagram

Hat
(Photocopy at 100%)

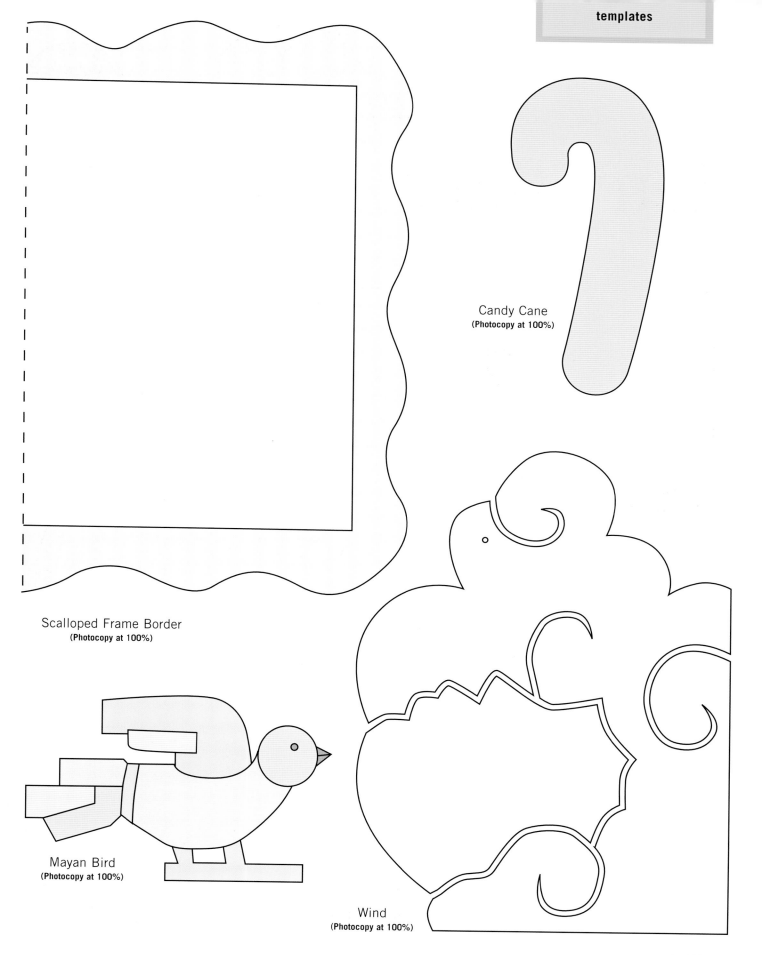

Candy Cane
(Photocopy at 100%)

Scalloped Frame Border
(Photocopy at 100%)

Mayan Bird
(Photocopy at 100%)

Wind
(Photocopy at 100%)

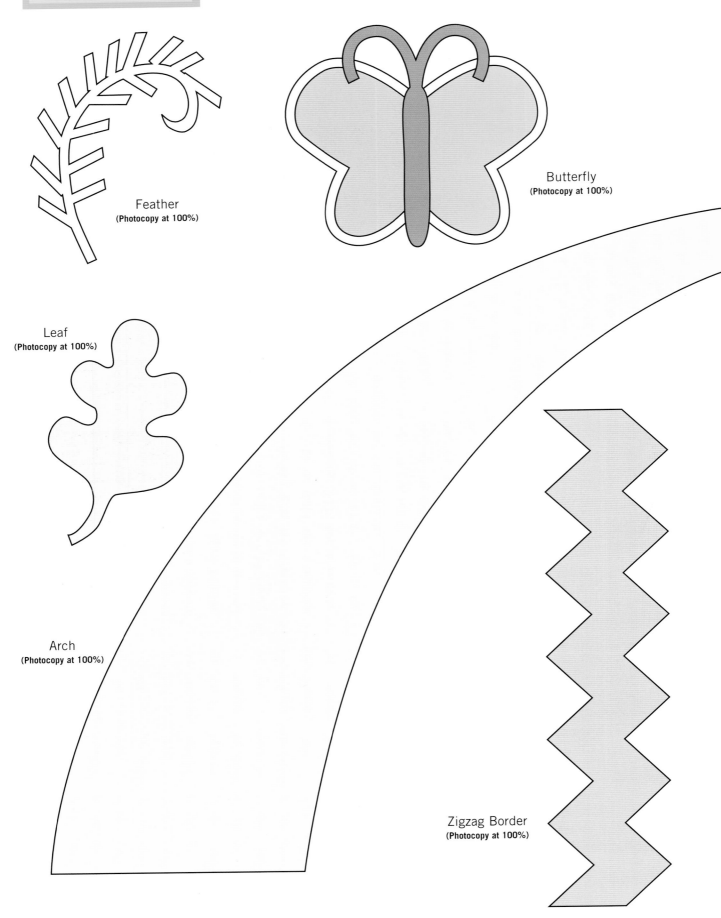

Feather
(Photocopy at 100%)

Butterfly
(Photocopy at 100%)

Leaf
(Photocopy at 100%)

Arch
(Photocopy at 100%)

Zigzag Border
(Photocopy at 100%)

Waves
(Photocopy at 200%)

Mask
(Photocopy at 200%)

Curvy Border
(Photocopy at 200%)

Large Heart
(Photocopy at 100%)

Spoon
(Photocopy at 100%)

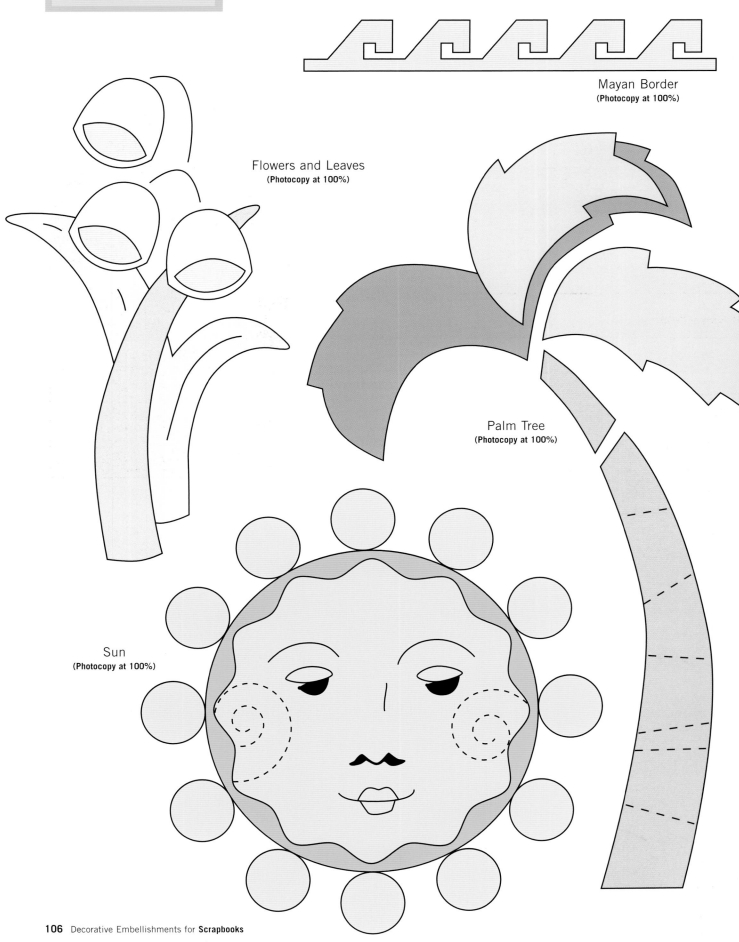

Mayan Border
(Photocopy at 100%)

Flowers and Leaves
(Photocopy at 100%)

Palm Tree
(Photocopy at 100%)

Sun
(Photocopy at 100%)

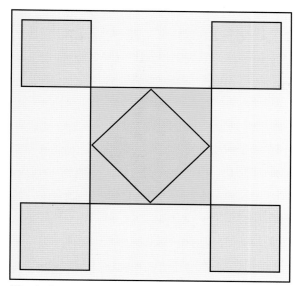

Block A
(Photocopy at 100%)

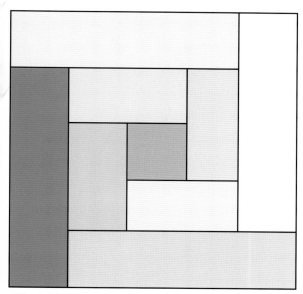

Block B
(Photocopy at 100%)

Floral Motif
(Photocopy at 100%)

House
(Photocopy at 100%)

Mat
(Photocopy at 200%)

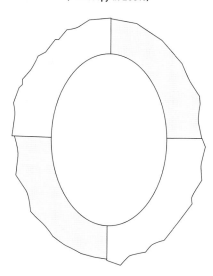

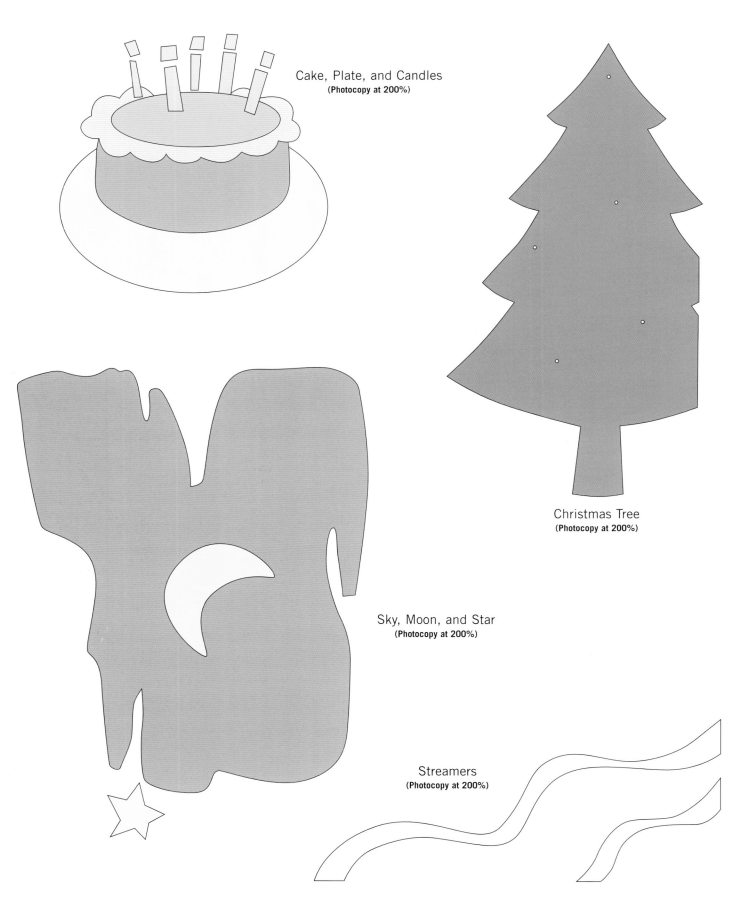

Cake, Plate, and Candles
(Photocopy at 200%)

Christmas Tree
(Photocopy at 200%)

Sky, Moon, and Star
(Photocopy at 200%)

Streamers
(Photocopy at 200%)

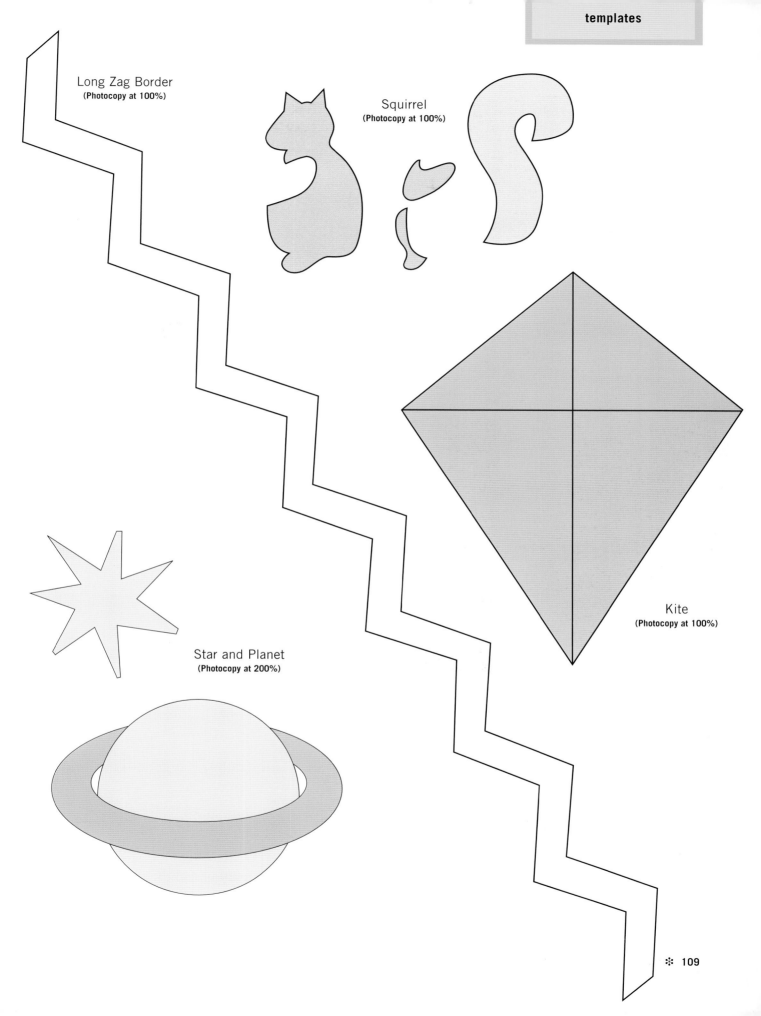

Long Zag Border
(Photocopy at 100%)

Squirrel
(Photocopy at 100%)

Kite
(Photocopy at 100%)

Star and Planet
(Photocopy at 200%)

❉ 109

resources

3M
(888) 364-3577
www.mmm.com
spray adhesive

Anna Griffin, Inc.
7333 Lambert Drive
Atlanta, GA 30324 USA
(404) 817-8170
www.annagriffin.com
vellum

Artistic Wire, Ltd.
752 North Larch Avenue
Elmhurst, IL 60126 USA
(630) 530-7567
www.artisticwire.com
wire

Aussie Scrapbook Suppliers
About.com
www.scrapbooking.about.com

Berwick Offray LLC
9th and Bomboy Lane
Berwick, PA 18603 USA
(800) 327-0350
www.berwickindustries.com
ribbon

Canadian Scrapbook Stores
We Love Scrapbooking Directory
www.welovescrapbooking.com/stores

Canson
21 Industrial Drive
South Hadley, MA 01075 USA
(413) 538-9250
www.canson-us.com
paper

Chartpak
www.chartpak.com
rub-on letters

Coats and Clark
www.coatsandclark.com
yarn

Creative PaperClay
79 Daily Drive, Suite 101
Camarillo, CA 93010 USA
(800) 899-5952
www.paperclay.com
air-drying clay

Darice
13000 Darice Parkway Park 82
Strongsville, OH 44149 USA
(800) 321-1494
www.darice.com
sequins, beads, craft foam

DMC
(888) 610-1250
www.dmc-usa.com
embroidery floss, pearl cotton

Duncan Enterprises
5673 East Shields Avenue
Fresno, CA 93727 USA
(800) 438- 6226
www.duncan-enterprises.com
glue

EK Success
www.eksuccess.com
pens, paper, stickers

Emagination Crafts, Inc.
463 West Wrightwood Avenue
Elmhurst, IL 60126 USA
(630) 833-9521
www.emaginationcrafts.com
paper punch

The Gold Leaf Company
27 Fort Place, 2nd Floor
Staten Island, NY 10301 USA
(718) 815-8802
www.goldleafcompany.com
composition gold leaf

Franca Xenia
Bedfordview 2008 South Africa
Phone: +27 1 974 8464
www.paperworld.co.za

Halcraft
30 West 24th Street
New York, NY 10010 USA
(212) 376-1580
www.halcraft.com
micro beads

HERMA GmbH
Ulmer Strasse 300
D-70327
Stuttgart, Gernany
Phone: +49 (0) 711 7902 0

International Scrapbook Stores
Memory Makers Magazine
www.memorymakersmagazine.com/locator/store

JHB International
(303) 751-8100
www.buttons.com
buttons

Kanban Card and Paper
Unit 1, Jubilee Court
Bradford Yorkshire BD18 IQF
United Kingdom
Phone: +44 1274 582 415

Lake City Craft Company
www.quilling.com
quilling supplies

Magic Mesh
(651) 345-6374
www.magicmesh.com
adhesive mesh

M.C.G. Textiles
Chino, CA 91710 USA
www.mcgtextiles.com
waste canvas

Memory Lane
1653 North State Street
Orem, UT 84057 USA
(801) 226-1159
www.memorylanepaper.com
paper, eyelets

Mrs. Grossman's Paper Company
3810 Cypress Drive
Petaluma, CA 94954 USA
(800) 429-4549
www.mrsgrossmans.com
stickers

My Mind's Eye
www.frame-ups.com
paper buttons, paper bows

Pebbles Inc.
(801) 235-1520
www.pebblesinc.com
wholesale paper

Personal Impressions
Curzon Road
Sudbury Suffolk COIO 2XW
United Kingdom
Phone: +44 1787 375 241
www.richstamp.co.uk

Plaid Enterprises
P.O. Box 2835
Norcross, GA 30091 USA
(800) 842-4197
www.plaidonline.com
silk ribbon, acrylic paint, stencil blanks, stencil brushes

Prismacolor
Sanford Corporation
(800) 323-0749
www.sanfordcorp.com
colored pencils

Ranger Industries
15 Park Road
Tinton Falls, NJ 07724 USA
(800) 244-2211
www.rangerink.com
ink pads

Rubber Stampede, Inc.
2550 Pellisier Place
Whittier, CA 90601 USA
(800) 423-4135
www.rubberstampede.com
rubber stamps

Sandtastik
(800) 845-3845
www.sandtastik.com
colored sand

Scrapbook Interiors
(888) 416-6260
www.scrapbookinteriors.com
scrapbook nails, paper tags

SEI
1717 South 450 West
Logan, UT 84321 USA
(800) 333-3279
www.shopsei.com
paper

The Stamp Doctor
121 East 38th Street, Suite 107
Boise, ID 83714 USA
(208) 342-4362
www.stampdoctor.com
eyelets

Stamperia
Box SRL
Via Orbassano 8
Vinovo Torino 10048
Italy
Phone: +39 011 9623833
www.stamperia.com

Therm O Web
770 Glenn Avenue
Wheeling, IL 60090 USA
(847) 520-5200
www.thermoweb.com
double-sided adhesive, fusible web

Westrim Crafts
www.westrimcrafts.com
handmade paper, wire, paper tags

X-acto
Hunt Corporation
(800) 879-4868
www.hunt-corp.com
craft knife

about the author

Trice Boerens has worked in the craft industry for 22 years as a
designer and as the author of numerous books and magazines.
Although textiles that feature needlework and quilting have been
a central focus, she also designs jewelry, greeting cards, children's
books, home accessories, and even tattoos. She has also done
design work for noncraft companies, including Warner Brothers,
Blue Mountain Arts, and the Bear Creek Soup Corporation. She
is a graduate of Brigham Young University with a degree in Art
Education and Graphic Design.

acknowledgments

Thank you to Paige Liljenquist, for access to her photo library, and
to Mary Ann Hall and Rockport Publishers, for the opportunity to
cut, tear, fold, curl, dip, stitch, glaze, shape, sand, crinkle, and
burn this collection of paper.